Smart Healthcare

How to Assess and Improve
Patient Experience Quotient

Data is the new oxygen!

Charles Bell & Greg Gutkowski

TO OUR STUDENTS

AND CUSTOMERS

THANK
YOU

John Elms

Nina Fazio

Monika Gutkowska

Ben Hill

Michael Lohr

CONTENTS

I
Preface

The purpose of this book is to:

A. **Establish a common knowledge** and understanding, among all professionals in your organization, with respect to technical terms and definitions of digital technologies relevant to healthcare organizations. There are too many buzzwords, vague defections, confusing terminologies, and frequently, unrealistic expectations regarding digital technologies.

B. **Describe the current status** of healthcare from a digital technology perspective.

C. **Paint a vision of Smart Healthcare** including superior patient experience by discussing what is feasible today, and in the near future, due to advances in digital technologies.

D. **Provide a practical measurable methodology** to assess and keep improving patient experience.

This book will benefit:

- Healthcare C-Suite Executives
- Healthcare Organization Board Members
- Health Foundation Board Members
- Healthcare Administrators
- Healthcare Policy Developers
- Doctors
- Nurses
- Medical and Business Students

A positive patient experience is vital to the success of every healthcare organization. It drives positive medical outcomes as well as revenue and profit. Yet it is very hard to measure it, and it is even harder to improve it. Such an effort requires a cross-functional, interdisciplinary approach blending marketing, customer service, digital technologies, medicine, and revenue/profit generation supported by automation and advanced real-time analytics and notification.

Today, patients, like most customers, are experiencing the 'Amazon effect'; i.e., the ease of searching and ordering with one click using pre-stored payment information. They get things delivered the next day and are updated about order status, shipment, and delivery with simple emails or text messages. They expect a similar ease of use, speed, and convenience from other businesses as well.

At the same time, the healthcare industry is one of the least productive sectors of the U.S. economy. A lot of innovation will be required to catch up with other industries with respect to the rapidly changing digital technologies driving the enhanced customer experience offered by other types of businesses.

Innovation is impossible without effective communication among key staff. Such communication is impractical without a common understanding of key digital technologies, technical terms, and trends.

Innovation is also hard to manage especially in larger organizations. This book provides a practical methodology to transform the existing status quo to a 21st century Smart Healthcare system.

1

Introduction

We are witnessing the confluence of five very powerful trends:

1. The growing cost of healthcare
2. Digital revolution
3. Rising competition for medical services
4. Rising customer expectations
5. Consolidation of hospital groups

This book discusses how to combine all these powerful movements to create a better healthcare patient experience while lowering the cost of medical care. It is a very tall order. However, the unprecedented improvements in digital technologies can play a big role in solving this challenging puzzle.

The aging population, ubiquitous unhealthy lifestyles (including the overconsumption of sugary foods combined with a lack of exercise), the growing cost of new drug development and hospitalization—they all lead to an unprecedented increase in the overall cost of healthcare. In terms of share of the U.S. economy today, healthcare accounts for 18 percent of GDP. In 1980, healthcare represented only 8 percent of GDP.

During the same timeframe, the cost of computing power (hardware, software, communications) went down over 10,000 times! The computing power of today's smartphones would have cost each cell phone subscriber $4 million per phone 20 years ago. In addition, we have witnessed the miniaturization of various wearable sensors. The best example is the Apple watch, which already tracks standing, exercise, walking, wellness goals, heart rate, menstrual cycle, loud noise detection, fall detection, and ECG.

Recently, the field of medical services has become more competitive, mainly due to very high deductibles. CVS is now offering walk-in MinuteClinics. So is Target in cooperation with Kaiser Permanente. MedExpress offers access to online consultations with a licensed MD, plus it provides an online pharmacy. Wal-Mart is housing Quest Labs where a standard blood test is $35 compared to the $150 charged by many current providers. Last but not least, the cost of measuring basic vital signs is near zero due to sophisticated wearables.

The fourth powerful trend is tied to the growing expectations of retail customers. This is especially true with online shopping. It is possible to order thousands of products with one click, 24/7, and have them delivered overnight at no additional cost.

Indeed, Amazon provides such an experience to its Prime customers. Today it is feasible to order these products by voice-command while driving. Alexa, which is built into Ford, Audi, Toyota, and Lexus dashboards, will gladly take your order. An email with order confirmation and tracking number arrives immediately.

Therefore, Amazon and its competitors raised the bar for customer expectations with online transactions to the highest levels. Since almost everyone has shopped online, we tend to expect the same level of customer experience from all other business— retail or commercial.

A medical patient is just like any other customer. Of course, the stakes are much higher when compared to ordering books online. In addition, patient perceptions are affected by their illnesses and thus make them even less tolerant of service hiccups.

Historically, for many reasons not discussed here, most healthcare providers have not thought about their patients as retail customers. Nevertheless, the best marketing and customer service practices of the most successful U.S. consumer businesses are very relevant in light of all the powerful trends discussed above.

Another trend is the consolidation of healthcare groups. Deloitte predicts that in the next 10 years, only 50 percent of current health systems will likely remain in their current status.[1] The major driver is cost-cutting enabled by economies of scale and new technologies.

This book, as well as the corresponding online course, provides a practical tool for healthcare executives to measure and keep improving the customer experience of their current patients. Thus, the methodology is called Patient Experience Quotient, or PEQ. PEQ scoring assists in the following:

- Identification of major gaps
- Estimated investment in closing the gaps
- Prioritization of closing the gaps
- Benchmarking with similar healthcare providers
- A communication tool for:
  - C-Suite
  - Board members
  - Foundations
  - Policymakers
  - Employees
  - Patients

---

[1] https://www2.deloitte.com/us/en/pages/life-sciences-and-health-care/articles/great-consolidation-health-systems.html

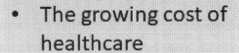

- The growing cost of healthcare

- Digital Revolution

- Rising competition

- Rising customer expectations

- Consolidation of hospital groups

2
Digital Revolution and Healthcare
I came, I saw, I digitized

According to McKinsey, healthcare is one of the least digitized industries.[2]

Despite using very sophisticated technology in diagnostics and treatment, substantial parts of healthcare staff use only basic or no technology for operations. For example, fewer than 20 percent of payments to health care providers and their suppliers are done digitally.

One of the major complaints of patients relates to the need to manually fill out multiple long forms asking for repetitive basic information such as names, addresses, social security, and phone numbers. In addition, patients want to have a single location that stores all of their medical history so they can access and control it at will. Another common frustration is the manual process of scheduling appointments that involves a long series

---

[2] https://hbr.org/2016/04/a-chart-that-shows-which-industries-are-the-most-digital-and-why

of phone tag messages, while other businesses offer 24/7 self-scheduling online. It seems that the digital revolution has not yet significantly impacted an industry serving millions of customers and accounting for 18 percent of our GDP.

The lack of basic digital tools to service patients is not only frustrating to them. It is also inefficient for healthcare providers as it ties up medical professionals with manual tasks. A major hospital group has found that "only 38 percent of staff time was spent with patients; the rest was spent on charting, walking around, and supply collection. In other words, healthcare does not seem to be productive.

It turns out that between 2001 and 2016, the healthcare industry contributed 9 percent of the growth in the U.S. economy—but 29 percent of the net new jobs. Put another way, healthcare employees are only one-third productive compared to an average new U.S. employee.[3]

There are several underlying reasons for this lack of productivity. Discussing them in depth is out of the scope of this book. Nevertheless, one of the major reasons is an outdated business model that lacks market mechanisms encouraging more productivity. Instead of prevention, the current business model encourages treating symptoms of preventable illnesses when it may be too late to

---

[3] https://healthcare.mckinsey.com/getting-right-care-right-people-right-cost-interview-ron-walls

address the causes. Another cause for lower productivity is related to legacy data systems and the growing cost of maintaining old technology in the context of IT budget constraints. The related problems are outdated manual processes faced by both patients and medical staff.

Additionally, due to the lack of tort reform, a lot of medical doctors protect themselves legally with unnecessary treatments, thus driving down productivity even further. Last but not least, the insurance companies decide what treatment they will pay without examining a patient. Nevertheless, there is great potential for improvements on three digital healthcare fronts connected by common data: automation and optimization of existing business processes, remote diagnostics, and new medical treatments enabled by digital technologies. Let's discuss them one by one.

Elimination of Paper-Based Processes

There is no technical reason for paper records in medicine anymore. Unfortunately, this is the reality today. The major disadvantage of paper processes is related to the manual recording of information. This leads to many errors due to false readouts of cursive, misplacement, damage, the lack of an automatic audit trail, and the lack of remote access, to name a few.

Paper is not a good media for such important and life-dependent documentation. Existing cloud systems with constant backups, redundancies, and privacy protection are better alternatives. Until recently, they may have been too expensive. Today the cost of making mistakes based on handwriting may be higher.

Procedure and patient scheduling is another time-consuming aspect of medicine. Endless hours on telephone-hold are wasted trying to line up the right resources in the right place at the right time. There is no technical reason for paper prescriptions anymore, either. Better data collection and analysis would improve clinical decision-making and reduce the need for redundant exams.

"A recent study revealed that medical errors are the third most common cause of death in the U.S. after cancer and heart disease, accounting for more than 250,000 deaths every year. For comparison, the number of car crash fatalities in the U.S. is about 38,000 and the number of murders is about 16,000 per year.

How many of these deaths were related to poor quality of records, duplicate records, or records not being available in the right place at the right time? We may never know, but it's reasonable to expect that a significant percentage of these unfortunate cases could have been avoided with better and more timely access to digital records.

The major benefit of the progress in digital technologies is ability and affordability of real-time measurements of all healthcare processes. We will discuss this very important benefit in more detail in Chapter 10.

Remote Diagnostics and Care Supported by 5G

Remote patient monitoring and diagnostics have great potential to provide improved access and quality of healthcare at a significantly lower cost. Nearly half of all adults in the U.S. (117 million people) suffer from chronic conditions with nearly 58 million suffering from 2 or more, and 86 percent of the total cost of U.S. healthcare is related to these chronic diseases. Heart conditions, chronic obstructive pulmonary disease, asthma, and diabetes constitute the largest cost component.

These conditions also have the greatest potential for using digital remote medical monitoring to improve patient outcomes and reduce costs. The federal government is already reimbursing patients for this virtual, "non-face-to-face" monitoring for Medicare patients for 19 chronic conditions.

The latest wearable monitoring devices detect key biomarkers in sweat and communicate wirelessly with a smartphone app. The device tracks data on wearer's pH, sweat rate, chloride levels, glucose, and lactate—high levels of which could signal cystic fibrosis, diabetes, or a lack of oxygen.
The existing Internet-connected blood pressure cuffs, EKG sensors, electronic weight scales, glucometers, spirometers, and other devices could be the basis for virtual care in real time. They can provide actionable patient information directly to

healthcare providers. Such information cab be the basis for individual patient alerts specific to their condition and medications.

Providers can set up nursing teams to respond immediately to changes in patient vital signs. This helps to avoid expensive and medically unnecessary readmissions while improving patient care.

Essentia Hospital in Minnesota has reduced hospital readmissions for congestive heart failure from the national average of 25 percent to less than 2 percent, simply by connecting an electronic weight scale remotely to the hospital's alert system. Weighing patients every day helps greatly to identify real problems. But coming daily to the hospital just to be weighed is inconvenient and expensive, so patients were skipping these basic diagnostics.[4]

According to a Goldman Sachs report, joining the physical and digital worlds and changing physician and patient interaction through digital healthcare "offers the most commercially viable potential to change the U.S. healthcare economy."

Goldman Sachs estimates over $305 billion in savings is possible due to three innovations:

- $200 billion from remote patient monitoring

---

[4] http://www.healthcareitnews.com/news/essentia-health-slashes-readmissions-po pulation-health-initiative-telehealth

- $100 billion from telehealth (remote diagnostics, counseling)
- "An infinitely large savings" from lifestyle changes to address obesity, smoking, and exercise."[5]

Here are some powerful examples of simple and inexpensive digital medical devices already on the market, all connected with each other and your smartphone that store and analyze health data in the cloud:

The Philips Health Watch can be used by patients with chronic conditions, such as hypertension. The watch shows users' steps, calories burned, active time, and sleep time. This $250 watch also comes with an optical heart rate monitor and accelerometer, which tracks varying heart conditions through an accompanying smartphone app. It knows when you were sitting too long and instructs you to stand up and move!

- 4 sensors
- Weight
- BMI
- Fat percentage

A $99 body weight device measures, monitors, and motivates users to change habits. It is built on the same Philips HealthSuite digital platform, an open,

---

[5] Roman, DH and Conlee, KD, (2015), The Digital Revolution Comes to U.S. Healthcare, Technology, incentives align to shake up the status quo. Goldman Sachs Global Investment Research, Internet of Things, Vol. 5. (June 29, 2015.)

cloud-based platform that collects and analyzes data.

- Blood pressure
- Heart rate

The $99 device measures blood pressure and heart rate. It's also integrated with the cloud-based health monitoring application.

- Fast measurement in 2 seconds
- One press of the button

The thermometer is $59 and is also synced with the rest of the devices. The wireless and connected glucose meter is available free from Accu-Check.

- Free from Accu-Check
- Integrated with smartphone and cloud

In summary, for less than $500 you could have a powerful mobile home lab for cardio, blood pressure, weight, temperature, and glucose recording, all conveniently stored, displayed, and analyzed for you. This is the equivalent of two or three doctor visits. However, using it and analyzing results may save you a lot of money, pain, or even your life.

In medicine, like in all other industries, Pareto's law applies; i.e., 80 percent of problems are caused by 20 percent of possible reasons. These four devices can help you manage 80 percent of your health problems for $500.

- Cardio
- Blood pressure
- Weight/BMI
- Temperature
- Glucose levels

And if you are diabetic, a fifth device may be all you may need to monitor your health without frequent doctor visits.

It looks like a super bargain to us. With the progress of 5G connectivity, doctors will be able to analyze real time read-outs from such devices

New Treatments Enabled By Digitization

The third category of benefits of digitization is related to new treatments and products enabled by progress in digital technologies. We will discuss 3D printing, robotics, ingestible sensors, nanosensors, and finally, DNA sequencing.

We will review the most interesting developments in each area.

3D Printing in Medicine

3D printing fits well with medicine. Most applications are precise, custom, one-off creations, and the speed and cost of printing is not a critical issue.

The most popular applications include custom hearing aids. An ear doctor will take and pass the 3D parameters of your ear opening to a device manufacturer for a 3D printing job. As a result, you get a perfectly fitting hearing aid.

Another usage of 3D printing is in preparation for complex surgeries. It is being used for the separation of Siamese Twins. The medical technicians render a detailed plastic 3D-printed model of the parts to be separated. Surgeons can then plan and practice the best way to separate tissue, bones, and blood vessels.

The next category of 3D printing application is in reconstructive surgeries. Imagine damage to a skull—the relevant parts can be 3D-printed and implanted.

The last category involves actual organ printing. It is now possible, for example, to print a new ear for you (in case you lost it or just want to improve your image).

Robots and 5G

Robots are the fusion of very powerful computers, sensors, and precision mechanics. They have a lot of potential in healthcare.

There are two major applications of robots in medicine.

The first applies to robotic prosthetics, which allow the replacement of lost limbs that can communicate with a patient's brain, thus restoring the basic functions of arms and legs.

Nothing can describe the state of the art of robotics and its potential better than this video:
https://www.youtube.com/watch?v=KPhkVPNKtVA

Another robotics application is for supplementing the work of skilled surgeons. A surgeon sits in front of a magnifying screen showing the patient while operating the machine's robotic arms with video game-like controls.

The robot arms can get into hard-to-reach places, cause less bleeding, decrease the chance of nerve damage, and reduce the size of incisions and scars compared to traditional surgeries. All of this adds up to much shorter recovery times.The higher cost of operation is offset by much shorter recovery time, which can save patients thousands of dollars per day in hospitalization cost.

With reliable and no-latency 5G connectivity, it is conceivable to perform surgery anywhere in the world as long as the surgeon's console can communicate in real time with a robot. In the future, all procedures can be taped, and all the parameters of the procedure can be stored in a database. This data combined with the data on surgical outcomes, may help in training and improvements in repeatable standard processes.

- Surgeon 'playing' a video game
- Robot gets to hard-to-reach places
- Less chance of nerve damage
- Less bleeding
- Smaller scars

- Faster recovery

Ingestible sensors

Proteus Digital Health provides a diagnostic system based on a smartphone, a patch, and a pill. Pills contain a one-square-millimeter sensor that is coated in two digestible metals. After swallowing, the sensor is activated by electrolytes within the digestive system. The signal from the pill is transmitted to a battery-powered patch worn on the user's torso, which sends the data via Bluetooth to a smartphone. Such systems can be used to analyze the chemical composition of the patient's digestive system in order to uncover abnormalities.

- One-square-millimeter sensor
- When swallowed, sensor is activated by electrolytes
- The pill transmits a signal to a small patch
- Patch communicates with smartphone

Another example of ingestible sensors is the camera pill—a miniature camera that can be swallowed. The PillCam is used as an alternative to standard colonoscopies. The miniature camera can detect polyps to identify the first signs of colorectal cancer. The battery-operated pill takes high-speed photos and sends the image to a device outside the body, which then forwards it to a computer for diagnostic analysis.

Nanosensors

The future may belong to nanosensors, or miniature sensors so small that they can travel in your bloodstream and communicate test results to your smartphone. They can detect cells that are shed from the inner linings of arteries—precursors of a heart attack that are hard to detect with any other tests.

This is a perfect example of what is possible at the confluence of major digital revolution drivers, miniaturization of sensors, ease of data transmission, and data analysis.

DNA sequencing

DNA is the essence of life. It carries genetic instructions played out from the moment of conception until death, and determines our height, intelligence, eye color, hair, what disease we may die from, etc. These instructions are coded in a DNA chain comprising billions of combinations.

Knowing our DNA helps us learn where we came from, how organisms are related, and how they evolved. In practical terms, knowledge of DNA is instrumental in finding cures for diseases, preventing epidemics, and last but not least, identifying somebody based on traces of their remains or to determine paternity.

If a Google search is looking for a needle in a haystack, then DNA sequencing is akin to comparing all the straws in the haystack to every other straw, and putting them in order of similarity.

Since a 'DNA haystack' has billions of combinations, it requires very powerful computers to do all this sorting, comparing, and matching.

Progress on DNA research is directly tied to the power of computers. This is a great example of the contribution of the digital revolution to the understanding of life and extending it (at least in the physical context).

In very practical terms, the knowledge of your own DNA can help in early detection of a possibly fatal but curable or preventable disease. It also allows for personalization of medical treatment. Today, most treatments are based on the overall result of clinical research, although when we know that individuals differ a lot in response to the same procedures or medications.

Also, most treatment decisions are based on standardized guidelines, using evidence from limited clinical trials. However, as the cost of DNA sequencing has decreased, some hospitals have started using genetic information to personalize care. For example, Dana-Farber Cancer Institute, based in Boston, uses genomic sequencing in 40 percent of leukemia and lung cancer patients to select targeted therapies[6]. Recent results demonstrate that genetics can also be used to identify patients at risk of steroid-induced growth stunting.

---

[6] https://healthcare.mckinsey.com/hospital-dead-long-live-hospital

Personalized care can be supported by real-time data capture. mPower, is an iPhone app developed by the University of Rochester Medical Center in Rochester, New York. It measures the patient's dexterity, balance, gait, and memory. This provides better insight into the impact of factors such as sleep, exercise, and mood.

Thus, we should be grateful to computer scientists as much as we are to medical researchers and doctors for advances in medicine ☺.

- **Better Existing Processes**

- **Real time measurements, diagnostics, and analytics**

- **3D Printing**

- **Robots and 5G**

- **Mini sensors**

- **DNA sequencing**

3

Smart Healthcare Aspirational Vision

If it can be conceived, it can be achieved

As discussed in the previous chapters, healthcare may use the most sophisticated digital diagnostic equipment, yet the processes preceding and following their usage may be manual, hence inefficient and error-prone. For example, a sophisticated MRI procedure may be scheduled manually, and the results could be sent via traditional mail. In other words, a patient may be waiting for 2 hours instead of 10 minutes for a very sophisticated procedure. In addition, the availability of results could be delayed by days due to a wrong address written by hand on a paper envelope.

It is worth noting that some processes, such as surgery itself, other medical procedures, moving a patient, food service, or cleaning a room will never be fully digitized. Yet they should benefit from the digital tracking of all the steps involving time, place, service person, and completion status. For example, a trivial and unreported delay in a room cleaning and preparation past 10 a.m. may lead to the room not being available to the next patient for the whole day. This may lead to delayed critical treatment and a negative experience for the next patient spending a night in the hospital corridor.

The Utmost Importance
Of Real-Time Communication

It is impossible to imagine any substantial improvements in patient experience without improving the flow of relevant information in real time. Getting real-time visibility to all processes is a necessary (but not sufficient) path to improvement in the delivery of services— especially for critical medical interventions.

Real-time alerting and communication became easier with the proliferation of mobile devices such as smartphones and tablets. Yet, the usefulness of these hardware devices depends on getting the right information at the right time to the right medical professional. For this to happen, several conditions have to be met:

- Depicting each step of every process in real time and moving it automatically in the underlying database can happen automatically in many ways such as by utilizing barcoding, RFID, or other sensors. In the case of manual processes, it can be done by checking off the item from a list provided on a mobile device. For example, a nurse can click on a button on a mobile app to check off that feeding of a patient has just been completed. Thus, the database would immediately record what service was provided by whom, to whom, where, and when.

- Assuming that all the relevant steps in crucial services are depicted electronically in real time, a healthcare organization needs to agree to the rules on who gets what notification and under what conditions. For example, if a patient complained three times in a single day, who should know that and when? Or if vital signs reach certain levels, who should be notified immediately (a nurse or a doctor or both)?

- Such rules would have to be coded to the system and each action based on them would be stored forever to serve as an audit trail for training or legal proceedings. In the future, Artificial Intelligence (AI) could also be deployed to address very complex rules involving multiple readings from multiple sensors.

- For all of the above scenarios to happen in real time, the underlying relevant and timely data has to be updated, stored, and maintained in a central location. This assumes the availability of dependable networks able to support large volumes of data. Needless to say, such data requires utmost care in protecting it from security breaches and violations of patient privacy. Blockchain technologies (explained in depth in Chapter 10) could be very helpful in this complex endeavor.

Data Is The New Oxygen

To use a blood analogy, real-time data is like new oxygen for the health of medical care. Like oxygen transported by the blood to every cell, clean data is vital to the optimal functioning of every healthcare process and organization.

Like oxidation that changes food to the energy needed to contract our muscles and repair our cells, data is needed to support real-time medical and operational decisions. And just like lungs clean and provide new oxygen to the body, we need digital lungs (aka databases) to provide a constant flow of new and clean data to our healthcare system.

Another medical analogy is also relevant here. Just like we use real-time vital signs analysis and subsequent diagnostics for human health, we need real-time data analysis and diagnosis of what is right or wrong with our healthcare processes. Otherwise, our digital system cannot be expected to do well.

Weak 'Handshakes' / Communication

It is seldom that an actual medical procedure is done wrong by qualified medical staff based on the information available at the time of treatment. It is much more likely that a failed or faulty procedure could be based on the wrong data or delayed due to scheduling problems or a weak 'handshake' between sequential and dependent processes.

Also, it is more likely that the lack of communication may play a vital role in causing problems after discharge from the hospital when the patient goes home lacking regular basic communication with their healthcare provider.

In other words, successful treatments need to be based on a mix of manual and digital processes. However, poor communication between the dependent steps may stand in the way of positive outcomes. Effective and timely communication is practically impossible without real-time data and information. Hence, real-time visibility into the status of all healthcare processes is of utmost importance.

Even if the data links are not broken, and information is instant, the processes themselves may not be efficient. This can occur when the right information gets sent to the wrong person. The best example of this is a call from a patient in a hospital bed regarding a non-working TV that goes directly to a busy, highly qualified nurse who should not be attending to non-medical issues.

As we have just discussed, today's healthcare systems may not be taking full advantage of the division of labor. Thus, doctors, nurses, and support staff may not be able to concentrate 100 percent on their professions. They may need to attend to a multitude of unnecessary manual and error-prone tasks taking away from the quality of care. The examples may include simple patient questions such as:

- When can I have my pain meds?
- When is my physician arriving?
- What's for lunch?
- What time is my x-ray?

A better way is for hospital patient requests to go directly to a unit clerk to be routed to the proper support staff. In addition, simple questions could be answered automatically with voice-enabled devices in hospital rooms.

Aspirational Vision
Virtual Care Center

It seems that the latest Internet technologies could be very relevant in addressing and solving these problems. As illustrated in the diagram below, a Virtual Care Center can fulfill many tasks remotely by the best-qualified staff.

Assuming reliable Internet connections and satisfactory protection of personal data, it is possible to house a medical support center anywhere in the U.S. and staff it with highly specialized practitioners equipped with superior communication software (audio, video, chat, data, voice to text, text to voice, email, and document management). This would allow for improved care management at the hospital, primary doctor's office, and home.

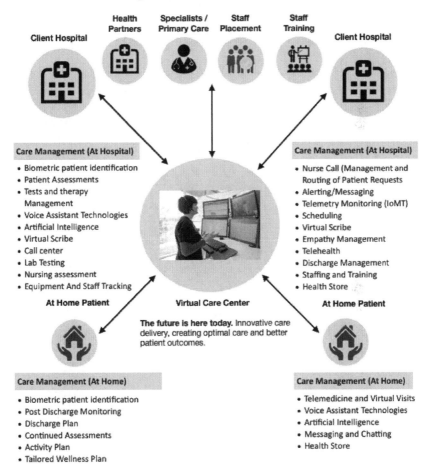

VIRTUAL CARE CENTER

Deliver the right care whenever and wherever needed

Client Hospital · Health Partners · Specialists / Primary Care · Staff Placement · Staff Training · Client Hospital

Care Management (At Hospital)
- Biometric patient identification
- Patient Assessments
- Tests and therapy Management
- Voice Assistant Technologies
- Artificial Intelligence
- Virtual Scribe
- Call center
- Lab Testing
- Nursing assessment
- Equipment And Staff Tracking

Care Management (At Hospital)
- Nurse Call (Management and Routing of Patient Requests
- Alerting/Messaging
- Telemetry Monitoring (IoMT)
- Scheduling
- Virtual Scribe
- Empathy Management
- Telehealth
- Discharge Management
- Staffing and Training
- Health Store

At Home Patient · Virtual Care Center · At Home Patient

The future is here today. Innovative care delivery, creating optimal care and better patient outcomes.

Care Management (At Home)
- Biometric patient identification
- Post Discharge Monitoring
- Discharge Plan
- Continued Assessments
- Activity Plan
- Tailored Wellness Plan

Care Management (At Home)
- Telemedicine and Virtual Visits
- Voice Assistant Technologies
- Artificial Intelligence
- Messaging and Chatting
- Health Store

Virtual Care Center Services

A Virtual Care Center would house the specialty medical teams and all supporting services whether the patient is at home, in the hospital, or at another medical facility.

The Virtual Care Center will collect all the relevant and granular data. All the information will be available for real-time analytics and alerting. The attributes of alerts such as frequency, recipients, content, and escalation schema will be established per procedure and process. In other words, it will be well known at any time who should know what, when, and how an alert will be acknowledged and/or escalated.

There are already examples of using digital technologies on a massive scale in healthcare. For example, more **than a billion people** are active users of the WeChat app in China. The mobile platform, launched by tech giant Tencent in 2011, allows users to send messages, make payments, play games, and do many other things—including, increasingly, take care of their health. WeChat offers a growing range of healthcare-related services: users can now book medical appointments, pay hospital bills, purchase over-the-counter medicines, and consult with doctors via chat. Tencent's digital platform gives patients access to the network of more than 38,000 healthcare providers who have opened WeChat Official Accounts.

And the company is continuing to explore new ventures within the healthcare space. For example, Tencent is investing in dozens of medical start-ups; it is also collaborating with hospitals to develop diagnostic imaging solutions powered by artificial intelligence (AI).

We believe there will be interconnected, transparent medical records that will be available to the people who need to see those records in the setting where they need to see them. So if an ambulance is called, both the paramedic and the receiving hospital will already have a very clear idea of who the patient is — in terms of medical history and medical needs.

Another part of the experience that will change in the near future is doctor-patient engagement. Today's technological advances are different from the computerization of the healthcare system in the 1990s, which drew doctors (care providers) away from patients and toward computer screens.

The next level of digitization will not be tied to a fixed infrastructure, so it will relieve doctors (care providers) of the need to be stuck to the screen. It will free up their time so that they can engage with the patient. For example, a doctor will wear a small microphone during conversations with the patient, and history-taking will be recorded and processed through the virtual care center using AI. Natural-language-processing models tailored to the doctor's style will pick up the important keywords, and the history will be structured into a data schema that can be used in the back end in the EHR. In the future, AI models will capture and immediately structure the data—it won't be the free text that we see in EHRs today.

Following is a list of various services that could be provided by the Virtual Care Center to support remote partner hospitals, rural hospitals, clinics, patients, and doctor's offices. It is worth noting that some of these services already exist. Yet we are not aware of there being a complex, large scale solution simultaneously supporting a variety of hospitals or doctor offices with a comprehensive program leveraging division of labor.

The following aspirational list is presented here.

Nurse Call
(Management and Routing of Patient Requests)

Nurse Call is a very important part of the patient experience. It's an easy-to-use remote-control-like device with clearly distinguishable buttons. This is where all patient requests are initiated and routed to the right service at the right time.

Nurse Call systems also provide Clinical Surveillance allowing hospitals to monitor patients by receiving live data directly from critical biomedical devices, evaluating the patient's status, analyzing Electronic Health Record (EHR) data, and applying customized rules (pre-defined by hospital protocol) to determine whether events are actionable.

This is a process that has already been successfully implemented in a central command center mode in several hospitals nationwide. In this mode, all patient requests are forwarded in real time to the Virtual Care Center. Then they are instantly routed using operators' discretion or AI algorithms. Needless to say, the patient's expectations can be met more timely and efficiently and lead to better medical outcomes.

Voice Assistant Technologies

Voice assisted technologies could greatly enhance Nurse Calls. Incorporating technologies such as Alexa, Google Home, or Home Pod utilizing voice assistants can address the following requests and questions from patients:

- I need a drink of water.
- What is my nurse's name?
- When will my doctor arrive?
- When can I have my next pain shot?
- What time is it?
- What is on the menu for lunch?
- I need help to the bathroom.
- And much more...

Alerting/Messaging

The quality and speed of patient care is essential. Otherwise, a slow response time may lead to negative outcomes as well as lower patient satisfaction. Yet, highly mobile staff at most healthcare facilities often cannot provide the best care possible due to inefficient communication. Staff members have become frustrated with the inefficiency that results from undirected updates and alerts being sent to staff members who may not need to know or act on them.

Only a unified cloud messaging/alerting system housed in the Virtual Care Center with configurable workflows will allow for real-time information to be routed to the right staff, at the right time.

Empathy Management

Using voice-to-text technologies will provide the ability to detect negative language spoken by staff members who are recorded. All conversations with Virtual Patient Center can be recorded and measured by AI. Management will have a real-time insight into the empathetic quality of conversation on the part of their staff. Bad bedside manners may be a way of the past if we start recording all nurses and doctors' interactions with patients :-)

Biometric Patient Identification

This is a positive patient identification platform that creates a one-to-one match between individual patients and their unique medical records, accurately retrieving patients' digital health records using biometric identification across all points of care.

Call Center

In the past, call centers were inward facing phone centers. Today, call centers need to be bi-directional and include omni-channel-leveraging web tools, mobile applications, texts, chatbots, phone calls, and email using the patient's choice of communication medium. Call centers are becoming *de facto* workflow management centers. Due to their centralized and digital nature, they are the perfect place to measure and analyze, automate, and optimize all aspects of care 24/7/365 in real time.

Some examples include the following:

Proactive Patient Engagement
- Outbound notifications/Reminders
- Outbound customer surveys
- Outbound calling campaigns

Intelligent routing
- Upsell services
- Service escalation

Understanding the Patient Experience
- Complete view of customer interactions
- Targeted customer satisfaction surveys
- Quality Management of agents and interactions

Workforce Management
- Scheduling
- Shift-swapping
- Shift training
- Agent messenger

Management & Reporting
- Real-time metrics & change

- Adherence to scheduling
- Performance management
- Call Recording
- Scorecard & evaluation
- Speech analytics
- Historical reporting

Scheduling

24/7/365 automated smartphone/browser-based scheduling with confirmation and reminder emails/text is probably one of the lowest hanging fruits. Mature technologies exist today to save a lot of time and frustration of playing phone tag with very busy support staff...and anxious patients.

Telemetry Monitoring - (IoMT)

Today's advancements in wireless connectivity, sensors, computing power, and Internet of Things (IoT) platforms make it easier and cheaper to build a robust, smart, connected infrastructure of medical devices, software applications, data, analytics, and services.

Internet of Medical Things (IoMT) which includes medical devices, wearable monitors, and apps that connect to healthcare information systems — has the potential to increase efficiency and improve our ability to support patients throughout the patient journey. IoMT can not only help monitor, inform, and notify care-givers, but provide healthcare providers with actual data to identify issues before they become critical or to allow for earlier intervention.

Telehealth

With the advent of 5G communication, the decreased latency and improved video resolution combined with real-time monitoring can substitute for most standard primary doctor visits, such as refilling prescriptions and addressing flus, colds, allergies, etc. We sometimes wonder what percentage of primary doctor visits could be handled that way. Our hypothesis is 70 percent, but research would have to be conducted to verify it.

Personalized Treatments

With more and better patient data, hospitals are also beginning to offer care options that provide more personalized treatments. For example, a Johns Hopkins team in Baltimore has introduced the Corrie Health app to aid with individualized recuperation after a heart attack—from discharge to recovery. The app allows patients to track medications and physical activity, as well as staying in tune with indicators for recovery, such as heart rate, blood pressure, and mood. The data is shared with care teams to aid a successful recuperation.

Lab Testing

Once a sample for testing is sent to the laboratory, automation reduces the risk of human error and contamination. Test results are delivered automatically as soon as available, and staff are

informed of abnormal results on their mobile
devices

Tests and Therapy Management

All patient testing and therapy sessions can be
managed through the Virtual Care Center using
configurable workflows.

Nursing Assessment

Nursing assessment is the first step in the nursing
process and refers to the gathering of information
about a patient's physiological, psychological,
sociological, and spiritual status by a licensed
Registered Nurse. Nursing assessment is used to
identify current and future patient care needs.

Continued Assessments

Assessments should be on a scheduled basis,
providing a patient on a regular basis with a digital
snapshot of where they are in their wellness
journey. Biometrics, Voice Assistant Technology,
and AI will play a big role in automatically
detecting gestures, posture, facial expressions, and
voice changes.

Digital Discharge Management
At-Home Digital Discharge Plan

How many patients, upon leaving the hospital,
remember everything they were told by their doctor
or nurse? How many family members, the primary

caretakers after a patient's discharge, are well prepared for such a challenging task?

The key moment when a patient should be absorbing post-discharge instructions to prevent relapse and return to the hospital is the very moment when the patient is focused solely on going home.

A simple phone app for patients and their home caregivers can provide individualized plans with checklists, video instructions, medicine refill reminders, and online training, as well as access to a closed online peer group of patients with the same illness (moderated by a medical professional).

This combined with telehealth and distant monitoring of vital signs could dramatically reduce hospital readmission rates.

Remote monitoring at home (including biometrics and live video) plus wearable devices will feed real-time data into a cloud service and directly into patient medical records.

With AI algorithms, remote monitoring may determine what type of intervention is necessary and notify the correct care provider for appropriate action in real time.

Tailored Wellness/Activity Plan

Wellness Programs help participants understand and prioritize their personal well-being: physical, emotional, financial, social, occupational, and even spiritual needs. There are many smartphone apps to manage wellness and activities. All they need as an input is an individual plan.

Health Wallet

There are already mobile apps on the market that consolidate all relevant patient medical information, activity, and real-time vitals tracking in one convenient place. Driven by API fetching the data from a variety of sources, they keep updating new information as it comes along. Then they share the right information with the right service provider. For example, when abnormal heart rate is detected or an abnormal trend is continuing, the right alert is sent to the designated recipient. One can think about the health wallet as a version of personal Virtual Care Center One.

Simplified Billing

Type in to any search engine the phrase *'help with understanding medical billing'* and you may be surprised to find the Wiley website's 'Medical billing and coding for dummies'. So now you need to buy a book to understand your medical bill???

Wouldn't it be great for patient experience to have a Virtual Care Center translate the convoluted and sometimes incorrect bills into plain English? And/or assist them to get the best financing options if needed including payment collections. Financial anxiety is probably not the best ingredient of medical recovery ☺.

Health Store

An online store for patients to purchase medical supplies and services provides convenience for the patient and an additional revenue source for the healthcare provider. With the uberization of the last mile delivery, it is possible to fill a prescription at a local pharmacy and have it delivered via Uber or competitive service while the patient is not feeling well.

Virtual Scribe

A Virtual Scribe Navigator – an individual located in the Virtual Care Center uses video collaboration technology to assist doctors and nurses with transcribing their live comments and communication and entering the data to the EHT system. For many physicians, data entry is a burdensome task that takes time away from patient care, so this kind of automation is extremely valuable.

Equipment and Staff Tracking In Real Time

As discussed in more depth in Chapter 10, RFID technologies are perfect and make it very inexpensive to track employees and tag every piece of mobile equipment in order to locate them when needed.

Staff Training

A Virtual Care Center can manage digital curriculum for patients and staff. In addition to traditional online courses, there is tremendous potential using Augmented Reality (AR)/Virtual Reality (VR) technologies to provide procedural training for most medical staff ranging from technicians to doctors.

With the never-ending changes in technologies, there is a need to constantly learn how to physically run specialty medical equipment. Prior to VR, such training was very expensive as it required an actual piece of equipment to be present. Not anymore

Staff Placement

Health systems are always in need of qualified staff for full time and part time positions. With the present and recurring shortage of labor, staff placement becomes even more important. A virtual care center can help manage this process.

Health Partners

Most hospital systems with specialty care, can partner with other facilities such as doctor groups, clinics, and other hospitals to provide specialty services using video collaboration technology.

Specialists /Primary Care Collaboration

With the use of video collaboration technology, specialists and primary care doctors can provide services to other facilities that lack these specialties.

Benchmarking / Center of Excellence

Virtual Care Centers will collect an enormous amount of data on a lot of entities, patients, procedures, and involved professionals. In addition to real-time tracking, alerting, and analyzing, such data lends itself to benchmarking performance. For example, a hospital group will be able to compare each facility on a large number of key metrics to help define standards and improve training and management. This should lead to improvement in outcomes as well as patient experience.

Medical Research

One of the major weaknesses of most medical research is small sample size and short duration. Imagine a combined multi-year longitudinal study with data for thousands of patients with information on diagnosis, treatment, medications, genomes, doctors, nutrition, vital signs, and outcomes to name a few. With the upcoming blockchain technologies, we believe that such a vast amount of clean relevant longitudinal data may bring great progress to medical research!

Security And Privacy

It seems to us that a Virtual Care Center could manage patient privacy in exchange for a small monthly fee. Just like banks guard our money, a third party can guard our privacy and make sure that our data is shared only with people who we gave a right to know. Blockchain technologies are very promising in this arena (see blockchain discussion in Chapter 10).

Virtual Care Center

- Nurse Call
- Realtime Alerts
- Empathy Management
- Call Center
- Telemetry
- Telehealth
- Lab Testing Automation
- Nursing Assessment
- Discharge Management
- Wellness
- Billing
- Health Store
- Virtual Scribe
- Equipment Tracking
- Staff Online Training
- Staff Placements
- Health Partners
- Benchmarking
- Medical Research
- Security And Privacy

4

Patient Experience Defined

No Patients – No Healthcare Business

No activity, regardless of how exciting, promising, or innovative, can qualify as a business until it has paying customers. It's as simple as that—no customers, no business.

Therefore, the job of every marketer is to get and retain customers while remaining profitable.

Introduction

Today's customers live in their own WWW framework; i.e., give me **W**hat I want, **W**here I want it, and **W**hen I want it. Customers are used to easy phone apps, nice website interfaces, online chats, overnight free shipping, 1-click checkouts, email reminders with enticing coupons, and friendly voice-driven support when they call a service center. If you cannot satisfy your customers, the competition is just a click away.

It was not that way before the Internet. Let's talk about the history of the monumental power shift away from businesses to customers.

In the past, you had to set aside time for shopping and physically go to a store or a doctor. With limited hours in a day, you could do only so much research. Your options for price comparison were limited. In most states, for example, car dealers lobbied for legislation to stay closed on Sundays, so you had even less time for comparison shopping.

Yes, there were catalog-based mail order firms like Sears, but the selection was rather limited by today's standards.

There was the *Consumer Report* monthly paper magazine, but it costs money and did not cover many less popular items.

There was no public forum to log complaints. There was the Better Business Bureau, but who would bother to go there or call before shopping for a pair of sneakers?

- Physical trip
- Restricted time
- Hard to compare prices
- Paper catalogs
- Monthly paper magazines with product evaluations
- No public mechanism for complaints

History of Power Shift

Enter the Internet and free, instant access to information on all possible products and their prices. Next, consumers started sharing comments and opinions on products and services on social media.

This put tremendous pressure on B2C (Business to Consumer) businesses. All pricing and product specs, as well as negative and positive opinions, were out in the open.

Next, we witnessed the proliferation of smartphones. Customers carrying smartphones were much more likely to tweet an angry opinion right on the spot as opposed to going home and having to do it on desktops after they had a chance to cool off. The feedback loop became instantaneous.

- Effortless Search and Feedback
- Effortless price comparison
- Effortless public, online evaluations of products and services
- Smartphone proliferation—an instant feedback loop

Amazon was the first to popularize the 5-star rating system for books purchased on their site. This was followed by Apple with 5-star ratings for iPhone apps. Both companies killed the proverbial two birds with one stone. They provided a valuable feedback mechanism to customers and simultaneously a tool to evaluate their suppliers.

Next came Google and Yelp using the by-then familiar 5-star system for local businesses such as restaurants, roofers, dentists, physicians, etc.

- Amazon > books
- iPhone > apps
- Google, Yelp
- Smartphone proliferation—an instant feedback loop

As a result, consumers got used to rating almost everything. This put businesses that had a lot of reviews with an average below three stars in real jeopardy.

J.D. Power has long been known for rating the quality of cars. Now they provide 5-level ratings by surveying customer satisfaction with the quality of electronics, financial services, healthcare, insurance, retail, travel, and even sports. With sports, they measure fans' satisfaction with ticketing, arriving at the gate, security, ushers, seating, food, beverage, souvenirs, and how easy it was to leave a game.

Consumers simply got spoiled with their power and with the ease of feedback. Therefore, today's customer service needs to be as easy to reach as possible and extremely responsive. In the age of Twitter, few customers will wait 24 hours for an answer. Easy-to-use interfaces on mobile phones, real-time chats, and Twitter support are becoming minimum requirements.

- 3 stars or less spells big trouble
- Twitter effect
- 24-hour response time not acceptable

The extreme ease of placing repetitive orders as well as providing data on historical purchases is a must as well. Amazon's Dash Button is a perfect example of simplicity in reordering—you can get your detergent with one push of a physical Wi-Fi enabled button stuck with adhesive to your washing machine. You don't even have to go find your smartphone!

- Repetitive, similar orders
- History of purchases
- Amazon's Dash Button

Customer Experience

This enhanced customer service is now referred to as the *customer experience,* as it includes all of the above plus esthetics and simplicity in the service interaction. All else being equal, a business with an ugly and hard-to-navigate customer support interface will lose to a competitor who put a lot of thought into making the interaction as easy and appealing as possible.

Customer experience blends digital and physical worlds, and it is a very exciting and growing phenomenon where we see a lot of activity and creativity.

Imagine waiting for service at a car dealership in a crowded, poorly ventilated, smelly, and poorly lit room with drab, worn out furniture, a loud TV, stale coffee, and no Wi-Fi.

Contrast this with the surroundings in your favorite high-end restaurant... The idea is to have a positive impact on all your senses; sight, hearing, touch, taste, and smell.

- Customer service vs. Customer Experience
- Physical aspect
- Positively engaging all senses

Good customer experience also involves managing expectations when the purchasing process takes time.

A great example here is a progress bar providing the status of your Domino's pizza when you order it online. You know when they put your pizza in the oven and took it out, and when the driver left the store. Another great example is FedEx's tracking number emailed to you when your order leaves the dock so you know when to expect delivery. You can track the status of Christmas gift arrivals just before December 25th.

Poor customer experience is very expensive

Most people like to travel, but few enjoy our airports. If there is a perfect example of poor customer experience it is security screening. Long lines, no benches to sit down to remove footwear, walking barefoot on cold and dirty floors, no benches on the other side to put your shoes back on, and indifferent stares from agents whose salaries are funded by our tickets but who forgot how to smile.

Actually, this negative experience keeps a lot of potential customers from flying, especially on shorter distances when the alternative is driving a car. So, negative customer experience cost airlines… customers. I know that airlines are not responsible for security screening, but their revenues suffer because of poor customer experience at the airports they serve.

Patient Experience

Healthcare is a perfect example where the blend of digital and physical experiences is very relevant. Digital experiences could involve attractive online promotions, ease of finding the right doctor online, ease of scheduling appointments, ease of getting appointment reminders, ease of paying, and ease of accessing important information including test results, diagnosis, and education about the treatment.

In the near future, patients may be expected to be serviced by robots for such simple tasks as food or medicine delivery. The lack of robotics will be perceived as a lack of productivity, hence higher prices and less reliable service.

While in a physical location, the patients' five senses of sight, hearing, touch, taste, and smell are becoming as relevant to a successful relationship and outcome as the digital components. It is hard to imagine a great patient experience in a smoke-filled room painted gray with a high level of noise, smelling of unwashed floors, and with stale food on old chipped gray plates served by a staff with a poor attitude. By the way, this was precisely the experience of one of the authors while staying in a hospital in a former Soviet Union colony in the 80's ☺.

Given the complexities of customer medical treatments, a new term was born: patient experience. A textbook definition is as follows:

> *Patient Experience is the sum of all interactions with healthcare providers that influences patient perceptions across the continuum of care.*

Please note that the focus is on *perceptions*. This is consistent with the marketing of consumer products and services whereby customer perceptions are more relevant than actual product features. For example, most computers provide the same basic functionality, but the look and feel of Macs, sold in their plushy Apple stores are perceived as upscale and distinct, hence more desirable. The same concept applies to Japanese car producers whereby the top-of-the-line Toyota or Nissan is hardly technically distinguishable from a low-end Lexus or Infinity, yet the latter are considered luxuries. In marketing, perception *is* reality and perceptions are very hard to change.

It is very hard to imagine a positive patient experience among unhappy staff. Therefore, every effort should be made for professionals servicing our patients to be satisfied with their work conditions.

Patient experience is widely considered a key indicator of clinical outcomes and organizational growth. The Affordable Care Act affirmed this connection by withholding Medicare payments to hospitals with low patient satisfaction scores, high readmissions, and other benchmarks. Improving the human experience of healthcare has become a top strategic priority for the majority of healthcare executives.

HCAHPS

It is worth noting that the healthcare industry has made an attempt to measure customer satisfaction. Indeed, HCAHPS or Hospital Consumer Assessment of Healthcare Providers and Systems survey is the first national, standardized, publicly reported survey of patients' perspectives on hospital care.

Here is a quote from the HCAHPS website[7]

---

[7] https://hcahpsonline.org/

"First, the survey is designed to produce comparable data on the patient's perspective on care that allows objective and meaningful comparisons between hospitals on domains that are important to consumers. Second, public reporting of the survey results is designed to create incentives for hospitals to improve their quality of care. Third, public reporting will serve to enhance public accountability in health care by increasing the transparency of the quality of hospital care provided in return for the public investment. With these goals in mind, the HCAHPS project has taken substantial steps to assure that the survey is credible, useful, and practical. This methodology and the information it generates are available to the public."

HCAHPS Limitations

According to McKinsey research, though, the evidence linking HCAHPS scores with clinical outcomes is inconclusive.

The reasons may relate to the problem discussed below in the Analytics section in Chapter 10; i.e., the lack of relevant data that explains what drives customer satisfaction.

The chart below shows factors measured by HCAHPS as compared to other relevant factors. It is worth noting that HCAHPS does not reflect such important factors as wait time, satisfaction with outcome, quality of food, ease of scheduling appointments, keeping patient informed, or room appearance. Hence, improving HCAHPS scores may help health systems increase their reimbursement or avoid penalties, but it may not lead to increased admissions and thus revenue.

In addition, HCAHPS concentrates exclusively on hospitals, although a substantial percentage of healthcare revenue is generated outside of hospitals, and fewer patients have hospitalization experiences compared to interaction with primary doctors and outpatient clinics.

Last but not least, HCAHPS does not address most digital interactions such as online access, quality of smartphone apps, and the quality of online interactions including websites, ease of payment, simplicity of billing, online education, or email/text follow up.

The following chart depicts many drivers of patient satisfaction that are not currently included in HCAHPS.[8]

---

[8] https://healthcare.mckinsey.com/consumer-health-insights-chi-survey

Many factors matter to patients

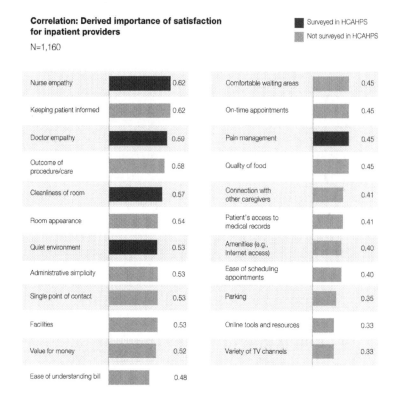

Correlation: Derived importance of satisfaction for inpatient providers

N=1,160

■ Surveyed in HCAHPS
▨ Not surveyed in HCAHPS

Nurse empathy	0.62	Comfortable waiting areas	0.45
Keeping patient informed	0.62	On-time appointments	0.45
Doctor empathy	0.59	Pain management	0.45
Outcome of procedure/care	0.58	Quality of food	0.45
Cleanliness of room	0.57	Connection with other caregivers	0.41
Room appearance	0.54	Patient's access to medical records	0.41
Quiet environment	0.53	Amenities (e.g., Internet access)	0.40
Administrative simplicity	0.53	Ease of scheduling appointments	0.40
Single point of contact	0.53	Parking	0.35
Facilities	0.53	Online tools and resources	0.33
Value for money	0.52	Variety of TV channels	0.33
Ease of understanding bill	0.48		

Note: Population includes all respondents with an inpatient visit in the past three years.
Consumer Health Insights Survey, 2013.

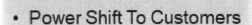

- Power Shift To Customers

- Amazon Effect

- Very high expectation

- Growing Customer Affluence

- Immediate Ratings

- Poor Customer Experience Is Very Expensive

- HCAHPS Limitations

5

Patient Experience Map

It's a Journey

Imagine a person relocating after retirement from the Northern States to Florida or Texas to enjoy lower taxes and higher temperatures. Or imagine a middle-aged professional family with school-age kids relocating for a job to another state. These are great prospects for many businesses, including healthcare providers—well above average income and education and very likely to be suffering from multiple health issues. Most likely the whole family will have to switch health insurance and find new healthcare providers.

For young families, Internet proficiency is a foregone conclusion. But older folks, too, are comfortable with the Internet as consumers—purchasing goods online, active on social media to stay in touch with family, and comfortable with Skype or Facetime to visit virtually with grandkids.

When they relocate, they will all most likely start their search for healthcare services online. This will be the beginning of their journey as patients.

Experience Map

Every patient or consumer goes through a journey made of several concurrent and interdependent phases.

1. **Promotion** - They browse the Internet looking for relevant information.
2. **Consideration** - They engage online while considering a purchase. They will fill out forms, make phone calls, download e-brochures, compare ratings on Google or Yelp, or watch videos to do due diligence before a very important purchase. They compare prices.
3. **Purchase** - They sign documents, make a payment, receive discounts.
4. **Service** - Their needs will be serviced by primary care doctors, specialists, nurses, support staff, financial advisors, nutritionists, or therapists. In healthcare, services include diagnosis, and outpatient and inpatient treatment, among others.
5. **Loyalty** - When satisfied with the service outcome, they come back for more services, creating a long-lasting and very profitable (for healthcare providers) relationship. They may receive preferential treatment as returning customers.

Today, most new patients will expect a great customer experience at each of these phases. If they do not, the likelihood of a long-lasting, profitable relationship decreases significantly.

Case in point:

1. If a potential doctor cannot be found online due to a poor website, the journey cannot even start.
2. If a doctor has been found online but the website is confusing, hard to use, does not have complete information, or cannot be accessed via smartphone, the likelihood of such a doctor to get new business goes down to near zero.
3. If phase 1 and 2 are satisfactory but the necessary paperwork is long and confusing, discounts are not offered, ease of paying or getting a line of credit are nonexistent—the potential patient may have second thoughts while competition is only a click away.
4. Given a choice, a patient unhappy with a healthcare service for any reason (various reasons to be discussed in more detail later) will be unlikely to return to the same doctor.
5. A patient who was treated royally during phases 1 to 4 expects to be offered special consideration as a returning customer. This may include loyalty points, other discounts, free education, online 24/7 support access, etc. If they do not get it, they may be less likely to be loyal or to provide good reviews or references.

So far, we have presented high-level phases of the patient journey. However, each phase is made up of multiple distinct, dependent, and repeatable steps. For example, the Promotion phase may include seeing an online ad, or billboard, or a mail flyer. The customer explores multiple promotions and the next step is to click on the ad, pick up a phone, or clip a coupon. In reality, these steps may be happening at the same time multiple times during the day and multiple members of a family will be involved using desktop computers, smartphones, tablets, and scissors ☺.

If a prospect cannot find your business, your case is closed before it is even opened.

Then, each step may be made up of multiple touchpoints. The same ad may be seen on different channels such as banner ads on websites, Facebook or Twitter or Yelp sponsored posts, various blogs, or email campaigns. From the promoter's perspective, the immediate issue is to determine what channels are the most effective given the same message.

In a typical patient experience journey, there are over 70 distinct touchpoints over 15 steps! Most of them should be dependent on Internet software and all of them should share the same underlying data. Following, we are introducing all of the touchpoints to highlight and further discuss the enormous challenge of coordinating all these neuralgic ingredients of success in a patient experience journey.

All the touchpoints form a value chain in patient perception. In other words, if even one of the 74 touchpoints provide a bad experience, the whole perception of a multi-step service may suffer. Case in point: a long, confusing, excessive, and incorrect bill will not help much to create a positive perception, even if the best heart surgeon saved the patient's life. The same goes for terrible food or indifferent or rude staff. Or for not protecting patient privacy due to lax security procedures.

Not every touchpoint will require the same level of investment or attention from the hospital staff. However, this is not about the hospital but about *patients' perceptions of experience dealing with a hospital*. Most patients are too worried about their health to care and/or understand the complexity of the process of supporting them.

All else being equal, if given a choice, they will take their business where they perceive their care to be fair.

- Value chain
- Perceptions
- One bad experience may ruin the relationship

The following table depicts a patient experience map made of 5 stages, 23 steps, and 74 touchpoints.

Stage	Steps	Touchpoints	
1. Promotion	1. Sees An Add	1	Online Ads
		2	Email
		3	Social Media
	2. Clicks On Add	4	TV
		5	Print Magazines
	3. Makes A Call	6	Billboards
		7	Radio
		8	Newsletter
2. Consideration	4. Clips Coupon	9	Paper Coupon
	5. Visits Website	10	Landing Page
		11	Forms
	6. Uses App	12	Ease of use/navigation
		13	Phone app usage
	7. Fills out form	14	Appointment Scheduling

Stage	Steps	Touchpoints	
	8. Schedule Appointment	15	Appointment Confirmation
		16	Appointment Reminder
3. Outpatient Diagnosis	9. Doctor Visit	17	In-Person Examination
		18	Remote Examination
	10. Diagnosis	19	Inpatient tests
		20	Remote tests
		21	Diagnosis
	11. Communication	22	Patient Education
		23	Communication
		24	Documentation
4. Outpatient Treatment	12. Procedure	25	Procedure Scheduling
		26	Procedure Outpatient

Stage	Steps	Touchpoints	
		27	Remote Procedure / Treatment
		28	Prescriptions
	13. Follow Up	29	Filling Out Prescription In Person
		30	Filling Out Prescription Via Mail
		31	Administering Prescriptions
		32	Follow Up
5. Hospital Stay Inpatient	14. Admitting	33	Scheduled Admission
		34	ER Admission
		35	Transportation
		36	Procedure Education
		37	Disposition Plan

Stage	Steps	Touchpoints	
		38	Sharing Information
	15. Care	39	Hospitalist Doctor
		40	Treatment
		41	Nursing
		42	Care Provider Education
		43	Communications
		44	Transportation
		45	Medical equipment
		46	Patient Advocate
		47	Auxiliary Services
		48	Pharmacy
		49	Scheduling
		50	Patient Education
		51	Mental Health

Stage	Steps	Touchpoints	
		52	Chapel
	16.Hospitality	53	Housekeeping
		54	Cafeteria, shops
		55	Entertainment
		56	Patient apparatus Convenience
		57	Room Comfort Control
		58	Room Maintenance
	17. Dietary	59	Meals Order/Delivery
		60	Meals Restrictions
		61	Dietetic Council
		62	Changes request by patient
	18. Discharge	63	Discharge Interview
		64	Discharge Plan

Stage	Steps	Touchpoints	
		65	Financial Services
		66	Transportation
	19. Billing	67	Easy to understand
6.Loyalty	20. Feedback	68	Ease of sharing
		69	Follow up process
	21. Sign Up	70	Newsletter
		71	Landing Page/Forms
	22. Benefits	72	Loyalty Points
		73	Awards (Discounts / Education)
7. Data Privacy	23. Data Privacy	74	Data Privacy

It is worth noting that this is a high-level map that does not depict all the possible types of treatments such as maternity or cancer protocols. The same concept of the patient experience can be applied by each department and reflect its specifics. Nevertheless, a high-level map is a necessary starting point in identifying the biggest and most common problems throughout the whole system.

6
What Is Your PEQ?
How Smart Are Your Operations?

Now that we have identified all the touchpoints, it's time to rank each one individually on how important it is to improve it. We will be using a 10-point scale with 1 being *'Very Important'* and 10 *'Not Important At All'* (meaning that we are very satisfied with the current status of a touchpoint).

Thus, if we are confident that a given touchpoint is of the highest standard and needs no improvement, we will score it 10. Conversely, if we believe that a given touchpoint is not even addressed in the context of patient experience, we would give it 0. For touchpoints that are addressed but still need improvements, we will assign a number greater than 0.

Given the 74 distinct touchpoints, the maximum PEQ score is 740.

The scoring could be done in two ways:

1. Individual self-scoring by executives familiar with patient service issues.
2. Group scoring by all C-level executives facilitated by an impartial facilitator. It has been our experience that this option provides the best insights into the strengths of operations of health organizations. Executives from different departments may have very different views and opinions on the status of each touchpoint. Most departmental executives tend to work in silos, but the issue is the overall patient experience as perceived throughout the whole journey. The facilitator will guide all participants to agree to a common single score per touchpoint. This leads to very interesting debates among executives and facilitates the creation of the badly needed common understanding of issues from a patient's perspective.

To use the online scoring template, visit 3clicks.us/peq

Stage	Steps		Touchpoints	Importance To Improve
1. Promotion	1. Sees An Add	1	Online Ads	
		2	Email	
		3	Social Media	
	2. Clicks On Add	4	TV	
		5	Print Magazines	
	3. Makes A Call	6	Billboards	
		7	Radio	
		8	Newsletter	
2. Consideration	4. Clips Coupon	9	Paper Coupon	
	5. Visits Website	10	Landing Page	
		11	Forms	
	6. Uses App	12	Ease of use/navigation	
		13	Phone app usage	
	7. Fills out form	14	Appointment Scheduling	

Stage	Steps		Touchpoints	Importance To Improve
	8. Schedule Appointment	15	Appointment Confirmation	
		16	Appointment Reminder	
3. Outpatient Diagnosis	9. Doctor Visit	17	In-Person Examination	
		18	Remote Examination	
	10. Diagnosis	19	Inpatient tests	
		20	Remote tests	
		21	Diagnosis	
	11. Communication	22	Patient Education	
		23	Communication	
		24	Documentation	
4. Outpatient Treatment	12. Procedure	25	Procedure Scheduling	
		26	Procedure Outpatient	

Stage	Steps		Touchpoints	Importance To Improve
		27	Remote Procedure/Treatment	
		28	Prescriptions	
	13. Follow Up	29	Filling Out Prescription In Person	
		30	Filling Out Prescription Via Mail	
		31	Administering Prescriptions	
		32	Follow Up	
5. Hospital Stay Inpatient	14. Admitting	33	Scheduled Admission	
		34	ER Admission	
		35	Transportation	
		36	Procedure Education	
		37	Disposition Plan	

81

Stage	Steps	Touchpoints		Importance To Improve
		38	Sharing Information	
	15. Care	39	Hospitalist Doctor	
		40	Treatment	
		41	Nursing	
		42	Care Provider Education	
		43	Communications	
		44	Transportation	
		45	Medical equipment	
		46	Patient Advocate	
		47	Auxiliary Services	
		48	Pharmacy	
		49	Scheduling	

Stage	Steps		Touchpoints	Importance To Improve
		50	Patient Education	
		51	Mental Health	
		52	Chapel	
	16.Hospi-tality	53	Housekeeping	
		54	Cafeteria, shops	
		55	Entertainment	
		56	Patient apparatus Convenience	
		57	Room Comfort Control	
		58	Room Maintenance	
	17. Dietary	59	Meals Order/Delivery	
		60	Meals Restrictions	
		61	Dietetic Council	

Stage	Steps		Touchpoints	Importance To Improve
		62	Changes request by patient	
	18. Discharge	63	Discharge Interview	
		64	Discharge Plan	
		65	Financial Services	
		66	Transportation	
	19. Billing	67	Easy to understand	
6.Loyalty	20. Feedback	68	Ease of sharing	
		69	Follow up process	
	21. Sign Up	70	Newsletter	
		71	Landing Page/Forms	
	22. Benefits	72	Loyalty Points	
		73	Awards (Discounts / Education)	

Stage	Steps		Touchpoints	Importance To Improve
7. Data Privacy	23. Data Privacy	74	Data Privacy	
Your PEQ Score			**50%**	**370***

*In this example, the average score per touchpoint is 5. The worst possible PEQ score is 740, and the best is 0.

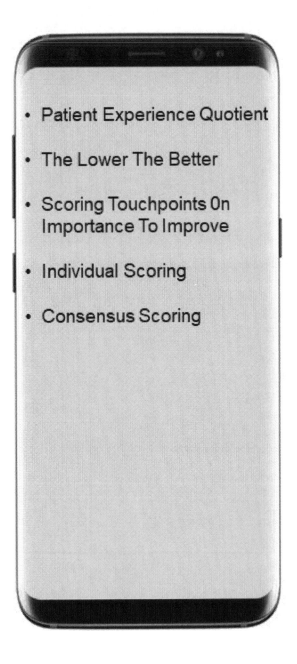

7

How to Improve Your PEQ

Identify and Prioritize Fixing Gaps

Now that we've learned about our PEQ, we also identified a lot of gaps or touch points—those with very low scores.

No organization has an unlimited budget or time to address all of its problems at once. To help prioritize fixing multiple gaps, we provide a way to assess the approximate cost of closing them.

Here again, we will be using a 10-point scale with 0 denoting *No Cost At All* to 10 for *Very Large Cost. No Cost At All* or 0 could be used to score touchpoints that require no improvements.

Sometimes it is hard to quickly arrive at the cost of improvements or to estimate them with a high level of precision. However, we can further prioritize the list by checking if a touchpoint is currently being supported by real time measurement or KPI. If it is not, it will be a primary candidate for improvement as it is very hard to manage without measuring.

The scoring can be done individually, but the best results are achieved when the score is agreed upon by a group of departmental executives.

To use online the scoring template visit 3clicks.us/peq

As an example, the experience map below shows hypothetical scores for Stages 1 and 2, Promotion and Consideration.

Stage	Steps	Touchpoints		Importance To Improve	Cost To Improve	KPI
1. Promo-tion	1. Sees An Add	1	Online Ads	2	8	Yes
		2	Email	9	3	Yes
		3	Social Media	10	8	Yes
	2. Clicks On Add	4	TV	1	10	No
		5	Print Magazines	1	8	No
	3. Makes A Call	6	Billboards	1	9	No
		7	Radio	1		No
		8	Newsletter	8	2	No
2. Consideration	4. Clips Coupon	9	Paper Coupon	10	2	No
	5. Visits Website	10	Landing Page	10	1	Yes
		11	Forms	10	1	No

Stage	Steps		Touchpoints	Importance To Improve	Cost To Improve	KPI
	6. Uses App	12	Ease of use/navigation	9	8	No
		13	Phone app usage	9	8	No
	7. Fills out form	14	Appointment Scheduling	10	3	No
	8. Schedule Appoint ment	15	Appointment Confirmation	10	3	No
		16	Appointment Reminder	10	3	No

The next step is to show all 16 touchpoints on a two-dimensional graph with the horizontal axis being *Importance* and vertical axis being *Cost*.

In this hypothetical case, we show data for the first 16 touchpoints representing the first two stages, Promotion and Consideration.

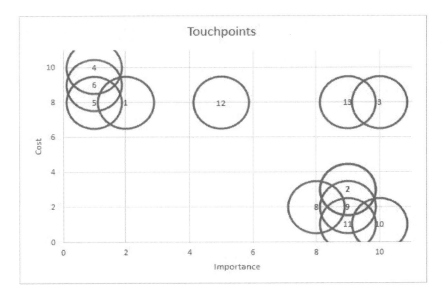

Such a grid will quickly show which touchpoints are the most important and can be improved at the lowest cost.

In this case fixing touchpoints 10 and 11 (Landing Page and Corresponding Form) are the highest importance but the least cost.

Conversely, touchpoints 13 and 3 in the upper right corner (creating a mobile app and beefing up social media) are very important but would be very costly to implement.

Such a grid can be the basis for defining a project plan geared toward the sequential closing of the gaps based on available resources.

The Importance of Consensus

PEQ methodology is also a great way to communicate with all stakeholders including C-Suite executives, board members, and various health foundations. Given the complexity of the subject matter plus new technical terminology, it is very hard to communicate with non-technical yet influential stakeholders.

Using the PEQ method, one can demonstrate management by consensus and objective prioritization. It has been our experience over the years that any complex technology project has little chance of succeeding without strong support from the major stakeholders—in this case, C-Suite, board members, and influential foundations.

- Prioritize Based On

1. Importance To Improve

2. Cost To Improve

3. Real Time Measurement

- The Importance Of Consensus

- The Importance Of Communication

- Variety of important non-technical stakeholders

8

Vision Implementation Challenges

Be creative with ideas, but focused and disciplined when implementing them.

Where to start, or what is the 'lowest hanging fruit'—It's hard to start complex projects because there are a lot of alternatives, each with its own risks. Alternatives can include selection of departments, technologies, most important problems, or any combination of these. How much analysis should one do before jumping in? Sometimes 'analysis paralysis' sets in and little gets done. On the other hand, starting a major project with little preparation is very risky. In general, it has been our experience that projects of this magnitude need to follow the well-proven Smart Design Process, illustrated below:

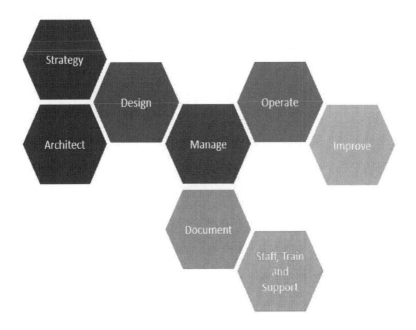

How to map existing and desired processes—In our experience, it is almost impossible to succeed with any process automation project until one gets 100 percent understanding of existing processes. This is easier said than done. In many cases, process knowledge is spread among multiple employees, departments, and even locations. Unless the process to be automated is represented as a well-documented workflow, the risk of proceeding is very high. Needless to say, one also needs to have a 100 percent understanding and documentation of the new process.

Getting consensus on scope and timing in the context of budget—Getting the project started does not mean that scope creep will not happen as it always does when the scope is not defined and managed. This leads not only to delays but also to unexpected budget variances. Such a combination has cost many executives many jobs ☹.

Focus—Staying focused is very hard, as every day may bring some new developments, including business emergencies, which can defocus the whole group. Achieving and sustaining momentum for large projects are very challenging and require a strong executive leading the effort.

Agreeing to KPI or Key Performance Measures for each touchpoint—The importance of this step cannot be overestimated. If there is no agreement on how the process will be measured in real time, the probability of success drops close to zero. With patients expecting reactions in hours, not days, it is impossible to manage patient experience without real time KPIs. If you cannot measure in real time, you cannot manage. It is as simple as that.

System Integration / siloed legacy systems—This is a major frustration for most larger organizations. They have invested a lot over the years in their IT infrastructure, but the technology landscape is full of old, middle age, and very new systems that do not 'talk' to each other on the data level. The relevant analysis includes asking the following three questions.

- Can your legacy systems support your vision?
- What can be quickly added, changed, modified?
- Does it support API?

API is probably the quickest answer to 'stitching together' the legacy systems with the latest patient-facing technologies. Yet being the quickest does not mean that it may not take 12 months or longer (compared to traditional system integration could take three or four years). Getting your legacy systems to support API is of utmost importance unless you can afford to start completely from scratch (which few do—other than new healthcare facilities). This is also the reason why brand-new healthcare organizations may have a cost advantage as they will not have to face having to stitch together existing systems.

An abundance of inexpensive off-the-shelf software—Cloud computing brought about an abundance of software, yet choosing among the vast number of choices is a challenge by itself. It is hard to select the right one because it is prohibitively time-consuming to perform due diligence on more than three or four systems. Given that most cloud-based solutions are relatively new, there is a risk that they may not do what they claim to be able to do. Sometimes even the software vendor marketing reps do not know the full capability of the software they sell ☺.

Sourcing and developing talent—It is very hard to find the talent required to manage and implement patient experience systems. The reason is that it requires the interdisciplinary skills of design, implementation, testing, and analyzing across various traditionally separated functions such as marketing, sales, clinical, support, logistics, and finance. Analytical skills especially are in short supply.

We predict that there will be a strong trend toward skills certifications starting with support staff, technicians, nurses, IT staff, and even doctors. Given the variety and constancy of changes in medical and information technologies, it is hard to know who can do what. The only way to manage multiple technical skills among a large group of people is to certify their specific skills and keep managing the pool of diversified talent. Certifications are very helpful in mapping a career path for new hires. This leads to better employee satisfaction and retention. It is hard to imagine unhappy employees providing a top-notch patient experience ☺.

How to measure implementation progress and how to communicate implementation status to a wide variety of stakeholders—Most important stakeholders such as C-level executives, board members, and health foundation executives are not comfortable with the rapid changes occurring in digital technologies. Nevertheless, their understanding and support of such impactful projects are of utmost importance. Technical jargon, buzzwords, and digital hype should be avoided at any cost. It is easier said than done because projects of such technical complexity are usually managed by very technical people. PEQ methodology addresses this problem by providing easy-to-understand documentation of progress, scope, and rationale for prioritization in the context of budget constraints—a language generally well-understood by senior managers.

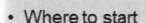

- Where to start

- Process mapping

- Consensus

- Focus

- KPIs

- Siloed legacy systems

- Inexpensive but hard to select cloud software

- Talent

- Measuring progress

- Communication

9

Summary

'If you can't explain it simply, you don't understand it well enough.' – Einstein

1. TRENDS

    a. The growing cost of healthcare
    b. Digital Revolution or very rapid technology changes in the context of legacy systems
    c. Rising competition for medical services
    d. Rising customer expectations
    e. Consolidation of hospital groups

2. DIGITAL POTENTIAL

    a. Better internal operational processes
    b. Medical IoT (biometrics, telemedicine, remote vitals tracking, wearables)
    c. New individualized treatments and wellness programs based on
        i. DNA sequencing
        ii. 3D Printing

iii.   Robotics

iv.   Text-to-voice chatbots

3. **SMART HEALTHCARE – ASSPIRATIONAL VISION**

    a. Leveraging traditional expertise and physical infrastructure via technology 'bricks and clicks' – Virtual Care Center

    b. The patient care journey: Primary Care – Hospital – Post Hospitalization

    c. Real-time tracking, alerts, communication, and analytics

    d. Data security and privacy – *who is going to protect it and how*

    e. Good news/bad news: the abundance of inexpensive off-the-shelf software, but choices are very confusing

4. **CUSTOMER EXPERIENCE EXPECTATIONS**

    a. High and constantly growing – *driven by Amazon and competitors*

    b. Supporting all four phases of care – *primary, hospital, recovery, wellness*

    c. Instant and easy communication is a must – *voice recognition, messaging, alerting, video, email*

    d. More interactions with patients must leverage patient smartphone

    e. Very soon, non – medical services in hospital and home will be provided by robots

f. Personal health education – *patients and caregivers*

g. Patient communities – *moderating closed social media groups for patients with the same illness*

5. PATIENT EXPERIENCE QUOTIENT – PEQ

a. Identify existing patient experience gaps

b. Prioritize gaps based on importance and cost

c. An action plan based on process mapping – *just digitize it!*

d. The power of benchmarking based on real-time measurement and analytics

e. Consensus and communication tool, share the action plan – *C-Suite, management, staff, boards, foundations, regulators*

10
Key Digital Technologies Explained
Complexity Made Simple

There is a lot of talk about the digital revolution, digital disruption, and digital transformation. We treat these terms interchangeably. In general, these terms refer to the impact of Internet-based software and mobile devices on our businesses and private lives.

Let us explain all of these concepts in plain English, stripped of marketing spin. We will decipher Digital, Cloud Computing, Internet of Things (IoT), Artificial Intelligence (AI), Application Programming Interface (API), Blockchain, Machine Learning, Text-to-Voice, Chatbots, Interactive Voice Response (IVR), Augmented Reality (AR), Virtual Reality (VR), Big Data, Analytics, Predictive Analytics, Business Intelligence, Data Mining, Data Warehouse, Data Mart, and Data Lake. At the end of this chapter, we will discuss Data Security and Privacy.

Digital

'Digital' in this case means any combination of software and data residing on a variety of interconnected hardware such as smartphones, tablets, desktop computers, and powerful computers in distant data centers.

'Digital' also includes any hardware that is connected to the Internet and sends data to another place. The best examples of these are home security systems, a Nest thermostat from Google, or smart electricity meters from a local electric utility. Medical sensors connected to the Internet would qualify as well—Apple Watch being a prime example.

Interestingly, these sensors will become very important in the healthcare industry, especially in the context of telemedicine. Today, in addition to monitoring basic vital signs, it is easy for these devices to sense vibration, temperature, humidity, lighting, and noise, among others. I can see a lot of opportunities to enhance customer service, not only for remote diagnosis but also for predicting telemedical equipment failure or need for service.

Therefore, when talking about *digitizing healthcare, we are referring to the concept of leveraging interconnected, mobile, sensing, and communicating*

Internet-based tools working together to increase business productivity.

Terminology associated with the digital revolution can be quite confusing. There are several reasons for that.

One reason is that technology vendors come up with marketing terms in an attempt to brand and differentiate their products and services. Given their large promotional budgets, they coin certain creative terms such as 'cloud computing', 'big data', or 'artificial intelligence'. The terms have become popular marketing terms, but they mean different things to different people and are therefore confusing.

The other reason is an attempt to describe old concepts using new terms to underscore the growing importance of existing phenomena. Twenty years ago we had EIS (Executive Information Systems), then DSS (Decision Support Systems), followed by OLAP (Online Analytical Processing), Data Mining, and finally today BI (Business Intelligence) systems. However, over all these years, they've all been doing exactly the same thing: analyzing data and creating and distributing managerial charts and reports.

Data scientist vs. old fashioned 'statistician' or 'data analyst' is another good example. Data scientist just sounds cooler, but the job responsibilities of analyzing data have been the same for the last two centuries...

Yet another example is Big Data, denoting just.... more data.

Cloud Computing

Conceptually, cloud computing services are similar to electricity production. Instead of every household having to pay for its own power generator up front, install it, and maintain it, we have a network of electrical wires connected to the local power plant. Then, we pay as we go only for the electricity we use. The same analogy holds for municipal water and sewage services. Instead of everyone having an underground water pump and a septic field, we have a central intake of fresh water and sewage treatment plants.

- Similar concept to electrical grid
- Municipal water
- 'Digital plumbing'
  - Procurement and maintenance of hardware and software
  - Computer networks
  - Access control & security
  - Data storage & backup

- ○ Redundancy for testing
- Business software

Cloud services are based on a very compelling value proposition. Instead of installing and maintaining software and hardware at your office, you subscribe to a service hosted on remote servers and accessed via the Internet at a fraction of the cost. This 'digital plumbing' includes the procurement and maintenance of hardware and software servers, networks, access control, security, data storage, backups, and a redundant environment for testing and development.

In the cloud, you could house all the software needed to run your business. In your offices, which could be far away, all you need is an Internet browser, a fast Internet connection, and a password.

Thus, you can just concentrate on leveraging the digital technologies in your existing processes and/or create new systems to enhance, for example, the customer experience instead of worrying about security, upgrading hardware and software, and maintaining communication networks.

- Compelling value proposition
- All you need is a browser, fast Internet connection, and a password
- Concentrate on adding value to the business

- Don't worry about the 'digital plumbing'
- Leave it to the pros

Cost of Storage vs. Amounts of Data

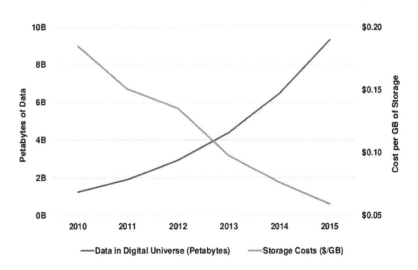

Data in Digital Universe vs. Data Storage Costs, 2010 – 2015

This graph illustrates the dramatic decrease in data storage costs over just five years. It went down almost four times! This is inversely related to the amount of total data on the Internet.

- Clever marketing term
- Distributed computing enabled by fast connectivity
- Specialization

---

[1]International Data Corporation 2016

- Economies of scale
- Very attractive, especially to smaller companies

The dramatically decreasing prices of software, hardware, and telecommunications is what made cloud services possible. Cloud computing is a clever marketing term, but in the technical sense, it is nothing more than distributed computing enabled by Internet connectivity. Cloud hosting companies specialize in providing all the 'digital plumbing' and, due to economies of scale, they can provide these 'services at a fraction of the cost.

This model is especially attractive to smaller companies that do not have, or cannot afford, a dedicated IT professional to install and maintain hardware and software.

- Great products at low prices
- The democratization of software and hardware power
- Everyone can afford the 'latest and greatest'

Cloud-based services brought about professional-grade digital technology solutions at very low-price points. In the past, only large companies could afford to buy and install expensive hardware and software at their premises, as telecommunication prices were prohibitive to smaller players. Software companies charged millions per installation because their costs were spread among very few customers. This expensive software and hardware provided a competitive advantage, because smaller players simply could not afford it.

Not anymore. The power of software and hardware has become democratized. Cloud software and business software vendors can now charge much less per user, as they can access a much larger user base worldwide. Everyone can afford a world-class CRM (Customer Relationship Management) system for $20 per user per month. What used to cost millions is now relatively inexpensive.

Here are the four major advantages of cloud services:

- Concentrate on leveraging digital technologies to generate revenue and/or cut costs rather than managing 'digital plumbing'.
- Trade capital purchase for monthly service expenses.
- Pay as you go. If you need more computing power around the peak shopping season, you do not need to buy more computers and then have them sit idle for the rest of the year. Just pay for temporary access to more computing power. Your total cost of IT

will be lower when leveraging cloud services.

- Have top professionals guard your digital assets. Today, companies generally need at least three full-time computer security professionals to effectively guard their business. Smaller medical offices cannot afford such expenses and as a result, a lot of them are highly vulnerable to hacking.

Good News - Bad News

- Eliminates IT infrastructure jobs
- Lowers the 'digital plumbing' cost
- Increases effectiveness and efficiency of business operations

Cloud computing is not good news for computer technicians that currently manage the 'digital plumbing' for their employers. Nevertheless, it is a very good trend, especially for new businesses starting from scratch, because they can concentrate on growing their business by leveraging the latest inexpensive software and avoiding non-productive technical challenges associated with maintaining their 'digital plumbing'.

The Internet of Things (IoT)

Think about the Internet of Things as a digitally connected world that includes houses and their appliances, cameras, buildings, factories and their equipment, cars, trucks, ships, drones, and airplanes—all being able to 'talk to each other'. In healthcare, IoT is sometimes referred to as IoMT, meaning the Internet of *Medical* Things. As one can imagine, the concept is about connecting medical devices to feed data to a uniform digital patient record. This may include inpatient equipment such as Nurse Calls, IV pumps, smart beds, or MRI as well as data from remote vital signs tracking, wellness progress, record of filling prescriptions, or biometrics usage (such as facial expressions).

Here is Wikipedia's definition of IoT:

> The network of physical devices, vehicles, buildings, and other items—embedded with electronics, software, sensors, and network connectivity that enable these objects to collect and exchange data.

I would add… This collection and exchange of data allows for remote sensing, controlling, alerting, communicating, and managing physical objects.

- Network of physical devices
- Remote:

- ○ Sensing
- ○ Alerting
- ○ Controlling
- ○ Communicating
- ○ Managing
- Over 6 billion connected devices In 2016
- 21 billion connected devices by 2020

According to a Gartner Inc. forecast, there will be 8.4 billion connected things in use worldwide in 2016. And it's expected to grow to 21 billion by 2020.[10]

A smartphone is a perfect example of an IoT node. It combines all these functionalities and more. Indeed, a smartphone is already a major hub for a lot of IoT applications including geolocation, tracking fitness and vital signs via Bluetooth, trip directions, speech and image recognition, remote control of home security and appliances, and chasing Pokemon, to name a few.

- Smartphone as a perfect IoT node
    - ○ Receives and sends data
    - ○ Senses location, vibration, altitude
    - ○ Speech and image recognition

---

[10] https://www.gartner.com/en/newsroom/press-releases/2017-02-07-gartner-says-8-billion-connected-things-will-be-in-use-in-2017-up-31-percent-from-2016

○ Video and voice recording and playback

A good example of an IoT application is the Navistar service alerting car owners that tire pressure is getting too low but is not alarming yet (in case of serious problems, drivers get notifications on their dashboard). The cost of sensors to measure tire pressure as well as the cost of data transmission went down so much that it became economical to install sensors on each wheel, transmit the data via satellite, and put it in an email to the customer. The same service would remotely unlock the car door if somebody locks themselves out (after the operator verifies their identity).

Other IoT examples include humidity and pH sensors placed in the soil and transmitting that information to agricultural irrigation and fertilization systems. The amount of water and fertilizer applied varies depending on the readings from these sensors. The savings can amount to over 20 percent of water, electricity, and fertilizer.

The ultimate easy-to-use IoT application, though very sophisticated behind the scenes, is a self-driving car. It is based on numerous real-time sensors working with each other to steer the vehicle in the desired direction while avoiding collision with foreign objects.

- Remote car diagnostics
- Optimal irrigation and fertilization
- Avalanche, mudslide alerts
- Self-driving cars, trucks, tractors, ships

IoT works very well when the benefit of monitoring and optimization exceeds the cost of sensors and data transmission. With the ongoing decrease in the cost of sensors and digital technologies, there will be more IoT applications. Some of them may even be hard to imagine now.

In summary, the Internet of Things is a big part of the digital revolution. It has a unique name to denote physical nodes sensing and exchanging information. However, from the process and analysis perspective, it is just another complex business process with a lot of data.

- Future applications may be hard to imagine now
- Cost of sensors and data communication and analysis is going down
- Marketing concept - not technical or analytical
- Just another complex business solution with lots of data

RFID And iBeacons

Here is an apt definition of RFID from Wikipedia:

Radio-frequency identification (RFID) uses electromagnetic fields to automatically identify and track tags attached to objects. The tags contain electronically stored information. Unlike a barcode, the tag need not be within the line of sight of the reader, so it may be embedded in the tracked object.

RFID tags are used in many industries; for example, an RFID tag attached to an automobile during production can be used to track its progress through the assembly line; RFID-tagged pharmaceuticals can be tracked through warehouses.

RFID tags can be attached to clothing and possessions and implanted in animals and people. In 2014, the world RFID market is worth US$8.89 billion, up from US$7.77 billion in 2013 and US$6.96 billion in 2012. This includes tags, readers, and software/services for RFID cards and labels.

A typical RFID tag will store a unique tag serial number, and product-related information such as a stock number, lot, or batch number, production date, or other specific information. RFID tags are perfect to track medical equipment, personnel, and even senile patients.

In contrast, iBeacon is a communication protocol developed by Apple to be used in conjunction with a smartphone. It is based on Bluetooth technology designed to minimize battery usage when in close proximity. The most popular applications include in-store communication with an iPhone owner by offering them electronic coupons relevant to the location they shop; for example, in a shoe department only shoe commercials and/or coupons will be sent.

The Common Thread - API

All software, hardware, and processes need to be connected to the right data behind the scenes for the overall system to work in real time. Think of data like oxygen in the blood, or as the common thread stitching your digital quilt together.

For example, when a visitor fills out a form on a website, they become a prospect. The data from the form should easily flow without any re-keying to an estimating and quoting module.

A quote should be automatically emailed to the address pre-stored in your database. Upon acceptance of a quote using an e-signature, the patient should be able to schedule the visit and/or pay a deposit on your website anytime 24/7 without re-keying redundant information.

A patient should have online access to treatment progress information, including all types of documentation. All relevant status changes should be communicated via the client's preferable means—phone, email, or text.

When the treatment is finished, the invoice is issued automatically and sent out together with a thank-you note and a friendly message that may lead to more business in the future.

To pull it all off, systems will have to exchange data seamlessly behind the scenes. This is where the API comes into play. The API, or Application Programming Interface, is just a tech term describing a standard way to exchange data between various Internet-based applications. Think of the API as a translator between various data outputs and inputs with multiple and incompatible data formats. Thus, a relevant analogy is an international business meeting of Japanese, Chinese, Polish, French, Hungarian, Russian, and Arabic native speakers. The only way for them to effectively communicate on business matters is… in English ☺.

Once the API is set up during the initial installation of software systems, it will sit in the background without requiring a lot of attention from your staff—just like your electricity.

Technology vendors not supporting common APIs today should be automatically excluded from your buying list as it disqualifies itself with the lack of basic technological vision.

Augmented Reality vs. Virtual Reality

Augmented Reality

Pokemon Go is a perfect illustration of Augmented Reality (AR). Nintendo added a game figure that appears on a real-time map on your smartphone. In order to 'catch' that figure, you have to physically walk to the specific place on the map. Then, using game controls, you can 'catch' that figure to collect more points. Thus, a new electronically generated entity was superimposed on a real map.

Another simple example of AR is the electronic visual trace of a golf ball's trajectory shown on a TV screen seconds after it was teed off. Without such visual traces, watching golf on TV would be much less appealing.

One of the neatest applications of AR is in retail when you can try before you buy. You can upload a picture of your room and then try different virtual furniture in the context of your current room size and decor. Or you can pick a product and preview what it looks like in any room through your smartphone camera. Houzz Personalized Planning is a great example of that functionality.

Another is trying on different virtual make-up before you order the perfect one. All you do is upload a picture of your face and try different products before spending a lot of money on cosmetics.

Augmented Reality is used on laptops, smartphones, tablets, and TV without needing special goggles. In healthcare, AR could be used extensively in training that involves placing objects in the right place or performing a task in 3D. Thus, it is perfect for medical trainees to better visualize real-life 3D scenarios they will be treating in the future. One of the most powerful examples involves overlaying MRI data on top of the body of a patient.

- Pokemon
- Electronic trace of a golf ball trajectory on the TV screen
- Try before you buy - Houzz Personalized Planning
- Virtual makeup studio
- Medical training and treatment support

Virtual Reality

Virtual Reality involves wearing special goggles and headphones that immerse the user in an electronic rendering of an environment that could be a reflection of the real world. A VR user feels like they're experiencing a simulated reality firsthand, mainly by vision and hearing. Examples include simulated underwater exploration of a colorful reef based on 3D color pictures from multiple sophisticated cameras. Or it could be a complete fantasy world of a medieval castle full of Disney-like 3D figures floating around you.

In healthcare, there is great potential to use VR for a variety of training ranging from how to operate and fix medical equipment, all the way to simulating complex surgeries. Since VR can simulate the three dimensions of the real world with the ability to move and rotate objects, it is possible to simulate, train, and certify motor skills requiring hand-eye coordination. The practical applications are countless, but the cost of training can be dramatically decreased. Also, VR allows for contextual training—only if needed right at the place of need. For example, when faced with unfamiliar equipment, a doctor or nurse can get VR-based instruction on how to operate it.

There are a lot of investment activities in this sector. In 2018, AR and VR start-ups raised over $3 billion in equity financing.

- Special goggles
- Total visual and sound immersion
- In medicine - perfect for sophisticated 3D training and real-time support
- A lot of investment activities in AR and VR

Artificial Intelligence (AI) And Machine Learning (ML)

Speaking of Artificial Intelligence and Machine Learning... We consider them to be just marketing terms. From the analytical perspective, these are just very sophisticated software algorithms used in conjunction with a variety of either very complex and/or voluminous data.

These algorithms require a lot of computing power or a lot of algorithmic logic, or both, to accomplish the task of optimizing a process. Algorithms are written by humans based on their business problem knowledge combined with their experience in computer science, and mathematics, statistics, psychology, linguistics, and neuroscience. It takes intelligent humans to deploy Artificial Intelligence ☺.

Is speech recognition an example of artificial intelligence? We think not. It is just an optimal way to recognize speech.

Several years ago, optical character recognition (OCR), or turning scanned text to data, was considered AI, until it became a boring but very productive routine.

At the end of the day, at the processing level, all data is just a bunch of 0s and 1s, whether it's photos, video, audio, text, or numbers or a combination of these. There is no artificial intelligence or machine learning. The intelligence and learning are in the development and implementation of algorithms that can take advantage of the available data and existing computer power.

> *Computers are incredibly fast, accurate but <u>stupid</u>; humans are incredibly slow, inaccurate but <u>brilliant</u>; together they are powerful beyond imagination.*
>
> *Unknown*

This quote is a perfect summarization of the contribution of humans and machines to so-called artificial intelligence, machine learning, and the digital revolution in general.

In medicine, these algorithms are perfect for analyzing millions of pixels that make up images (MRI, scans, X-Rays, etc.). One can 'teach' an algorithm to diagnose malignant cancer from images. The success rate of algorithmic diagnosis already exceeds that of a highly trained MD pathologist.

- Require powerful algorithms
- May require a lot of computing power
- Written by humans
- Just another optimization process
- Intelligence is in writing and implementing algorithms
- In medicine, image-based recognition to diagnose illness

Big Data

Big Data is just a marketing term used to draw attention to the issues associated with the technical challenges related to the management of very large data sets that are quickly updated and contain various types of unstructured data.

Big Data denotes just.... more data ☺

The popular term *Big Data* was coined by META Group (now Gartner, an IT research company) to describe data sets that have:

1. High volume
2. High velocity
3. High variety

High volume means a lot of data in relation to what we used in the past (but META Group did not define how much data makes it 'big'); high velocity, which means high speed or real-time data inputs and outputs; and variety, which refers to the range of data types (unstructured text and numerics from emails and posts, images, video, audio). Facebook data on 1.7 billion users would surely fit that definition.

In the not so distant past, most of the data to be analyzed was structured in rows and columns (think Excel) and did not change in real-time (it was updated daily, weekly, or monthly). One exception is the high-speed transaction processing used by banks and large financial institutions; but even this doesn't meet the variety test. Today, data also comes from a variety of sources and keeps changing non-stop in real-time.

- Definition of 'Big' by Meta Group
  - High volume
  - High velocity - lots of updates in real-time
  - High variety - text, image, video, audio

- Marketing term
- Drawing attention to the challenges of managing very large databases
- In the past, most data was just numbers in neat rows and columns

Data, whether big or small, is the foundation of all business transactions and the *de facto* new business currency. It is the digital glue of the digital disruption, the digitization of existing processes, and the creation of new products and services. All of these require a lot of data to work well. They also generate lots of data.

- New business currency
- Digital glue of digital revolution, which ...needs a lot of data and...
- ...generates a lot of data

The best examples of big data are social media platforms that are both data-hungry and data-intensive. Their success is based on the ability to collect as much relevant data as they can so they can sell it to advertisers. Their value is directly proportional to the number of users and their activities—hence data. Imagine the technical complexity of managing Facebook data generated by more than 1.7 billion users, constantly creating and sharing enormous amounts of new content globally.

Another example is an e-commerce site. To build an e-commerce site, we need product data, communication data, security data, and the room to store all future transaction data. Next, we need customer data to design and implement a marketing campaign. Then we start collecting all the web traffic data, data on the behaviors of visitors and prospects on our website before they decided to buy, and then transaction data after the actual sale. Finally, we need fulfillment data, shipment data, and returns data, to name a few. Imagine the amount of data behind Amazon's e-commerce site, which sells 480 million different products.

Internet of Things applications tend to create a lot of data as well. Imagine thousands of sensors residing on an oil platform sending measurement results to a central processor every millisecond.

- Social media
- E-commerce
- The Internet of Things

From an analytical perspective, the amount of data may be irrelevant to the process of discovery of patterns in the data. Actually, a lot of valid research can be done on a good sample of data. We do not always need all of the data to draw statistically valid conclusions. Also, more data does not necessarily mean better data—especially if it is incorrect, irrelevant, or incomplete.

However, we need all data when we want to summarize all transactions or do detailed reports broken down by various categories such as procedure, department, patient, etc.

- Bigger does not mean better
- Can do research on sample data
- Need all data for summaries and management reports

Data Warehouse, Data Mart, Data Lake

Data Warehouse is a term used to denote the functional scope and physical space where certain business data is stored. A Data Warehouse usually stores data belonging to a particular business department. Data Warehouse is just a marketing term applied to large business databases.

Conceptually, Big Data may reside in a Data Warehouse.

- Databases organized by business function
  - Revenue Data Warehouse

- ○ Marketing Data Warehouse
- ○ Financial Data Warehouse

- Marketing Data Warehouse may be made up of
  - ○ Social Media Data Mart
  - ○ Web Traffic Data Mart
  - ○ Online Advertising Data Mart
  - ○
- From a technical and analytical perspective, they are just databases.

Companies now maintain a Sales/Revenue Data Warehouse, a Financial Data Warehouse, or a Marketing Data Warehouse (or Mart or Lake) denoting the scope of their logical functionality.

'Marts' and 'Lakes' usually denote smaller databases or logical subsets of larger entities. Thus, the Marketing Data Warehouse can be made up of a Social Media Data Mart (or Lake) and a Web Traffic Data Mart (or Lake).

If vendors continue along these lines of naming conventions, we may soon have Data Pools, Data Ponds, and Data Puddles ☺.

From the technical and analytical perspective, these terms are completely irrelevant. Data analysis always included queries against databases, regardless of how they are named, how they related to each other, or how big they were.

Blockchain

Tracking health status as well as medical services, procedures, and meds for every individual over their lifetime is a very complex task perfectly suited to a blockchain application. Blockchain is just a fancy name for organizing the data while ensuring its quality and thus increasing the trust in utilizing it for important decisions.

Imagine an Excel spreadsheet while inputting rows of data. Excel can be programmed to check if the new row of data is consistent with the previous one. If it is not, one cannot add a new row of data. The rules for consistency are defined by specialists. This eliminates most errors that would be otherwise very hard to catch.

Imagine a newborn today getting on a health blockchain from day one (or an encrypted, safe, and reliable personal database). All of the baby's data would be stored there. Any additional data could only be appended after an integrity check with the previous block. So, for example, if a baby is found to have an allergy to penicillin, a new block will not be added if it includes a prescription for penicillin.

Or a new block will be rejected if the height is 200 percent of the height measured just a month ago (babies do not grow that fast :-). It sounds simple, but it takes a lot of computing power to check all the rules before allowing new data to be entered when dealing with billions of records.

Going forward, every piece of health data could be stored in a blockchain. This may include readings from Fitbits, smart-watches, gyms, smart beds, nutrition systems, or diagnostic equipment. This may include all medicines purchased (not just prescribed), as well as financial charges, thus enabling automatic invoicing/billing without having to spend days and hours to check its integrity.

The major benefit of blockchain is the automation of trust. Due to stringent data quality controls (which can be easily audited), we will be able to trust the information in the database even in the life-and-death situations. This will allow the automation of a lot of medical and clerical processes that today require human intervention.

By the way, effective blockchain assumes total privacy protection and the right of a patient to disclose the information only at their discretion amidst strong due diligence processes.

The value of such data cannot be overestimated. It will help in prevention management and thus prolong the life of individuals. It will provide enormous value to clinical trials and medical research. Thus, it has the potential to lower the total cost of medical care worldwide.

In general, the more transparency and trust, the lower the cost of doing business. There are several ways transparency contributes to lower cost:

1. Less time and energy wasted on checking, cross-checking, double-checking, guessing, analyzing, and fire-fighting—and more time for value-add tasks.
2. Prevention of problems not known today. The cost of *not knowing what you don't know* can be greatly reduced. No mental drain anticipating problems—everything is accounted for. Many managers complain that *not knowing what they don't know* is one of the most frustrating parts of their jobs. It is hard to work knowing that unknown problems could come out of nowhere at any time, and it is almost impossible to anticipate them all.
3. Better, more relevant process data. Thus, we can use better analytics that will lead to process improvement and better resource allocation. This is huge by itself; today, poor

data quality and/or missing information preclude a lot of preventive discoveries.

4. Automation of clerical tasks such as ordering, invoicing, dispatching, calling, and emailing.
5. Better and more timely communication with patients. We are more likely to retain the best patients if our communication is more timely and of higher quality than the competition.

A good blockchain application should increase trust in the process and reduce cost as well as the anxieties associated with it. Here is a high-level summary of the benefits of using blockchain technologies in business processes:

1. Real-time tracking of relevant information
2. Real-time problem prevention - No more *I don't know what I don't know*
3. Real-time communication of relevant information
4. Automation of documentation
5. Automation of most clerical tasks
6. Increased quality of data for analysis, prevention, and optimization
7. Lower cost of labor, transportation, and support functions per project

Voice to Text - Chatbots and IVRs

Today, it is possible to turn voice into text in real time with 95 percent precision. With the trend toward using voice to search the Internet and communicate with Internet applications—Alexa being a prime example—we anticipate that the importance of call centers will grow.

Imagine a simple scenario where a person verbally requests the address of the nearest hospital while driving. Such a call can be easily turned to text by a computer and then the search will happen in a traditional way based on provided text. This automatic conversion is done by technology called *chatbot*. The address can be provided back to a driver by chatbot as well via voice, or passed directly to their GPS or both. Chatbots are useful for both voice chats as well as chats typed on websites.

For such a simple question, the answer can be automated. However, not all chatbot questions will be that simple. The challenge is in learning what percentage of calls can be automated to save time and provide training for live agents. The more sophisticated chatbots could answer a higher percentage of questions or collect more data via voice. One way or another, they will have to be mapped to IVR or Interactive Voice Response algorithms of the call center software to provide automatic answers.

Let me give you an example. Imagine a help line for a distributor of medical electronic equipment. A chatbot can be set up to help a caller with a diagnosis of equipment failure. The initial questions can be answered *yes* or *no*. These questions can ask the name of the equipment, if it is plugged in, if the light on the front is illuminated, and if the equipment is hot. Only if a customer answers *no* to the last three questions will the IVR will route the call to an agent who specializes in servicing a given piece of equipment. Conversely, if a customer answers any of the last three questions *yes* will the chatbot recommend the next diagnostic steps.

In addition, voice-to-text in real time also enables service quality monitoring in real time. By analyzing the type of words used by an agent or a customer, the call center manager can be alerted in real time about a contentious conversation whereby a lot of expressions are used such as *I am frustrated, I hate your product,* or *Why is it so hard to use it?* A computer can also detect swear words used by either party. Needless to say, the manager can learn whether the problem is with the client, agent, or both. The results of this analysis could be used for better training of agents facing unreasonable or aggressive customers or sick patients.

Analytics

Analytics = Analysis = Data Analysis = Business Analytics = Business Analysis

We define data analysis as the process of discovering useful information from data to support decision-making. Like with many terms in the digital world, this one also overlaps with other frequently used terms such as statistics, data mining, data modeling, and data visualization.

Real-time analytics are of extreme importance in healthcare where split-second decisions have to be made. Blockchain applications will provide trusted real-time data, thus increasing the importance of analytics in practicing medicine.

Analytics are based on measurements. Digital technologies just make measuring more frequent, more granular, and more accurate. At the end of the day, we are witnessing a measurement revolution enabled by technology. Technology by itself is just a tool and of little value if not used to measure to support making decisions. Yet a lot of media hype is about the digital technology itself.

Statistics vs. Analytics

- Statistics: 30+20=50

- Analytics: We admitted 50 patients in the last 2 years, but last year admissions went down 33%

If you think about statistics as data science, think about data analytics as a practical application of data science in business decision-making. Analytics is the application of statistics to real problem-solving.

A good example of the differences between statistics and business analytics is presented here:

Statistics: 30 +20 =50. In the abstract, this is just pure math: if you add 30 to 20 you get 50.

Analytics: If 30 represents the number of patients last year and 20 represents current year patients, then the more meaningful number is that we admitted fewer patients—ten fewer (30-20=10) or 33 percent fewer than last year (10/30*100=33%) compared to the fact that in two years we admitted 50 patients. Most healthcare managers would likely be concerned about a 33 percent drop in admissions in one year as compared to total admissions over two years.

Effective Analytics

- Is it good or bad or indifferent?

- o Revenue does not mean profit
  - o What was the goal?
  - o What was the competitive landscape?
  - o What were the bonuses based on?

- Need to know very well:
  - o Business context
  - o Market
  - o Products
  - o Competition
  - o Corporate goals
  - o Corporate politics

Are these business results good or bad or indifferent? This depends on a manager's goals and responsibilities. Maybe the plan was to admit 40 patients in two years and now they are 10 patients ahead of the goal. Or maybe fewer patients were admitted the second year but at a much higher profit per patient. Or maybe the competition introduced a better product and few would have been able to admit 30 patients for a given procedure in the second year.

Was the manager's incentive bonus tied to the number of patients, revenue, profitability, or market share? And so on and so forth…. Thus, business analysis is impossible to get right without an intimate knowledge of products, revenue goals, market conditions, competitors' actions, corporate politics, etc.

This is why meaningful business analysis cannot be left to scientists or statisticians focused on statistics and math only.

- Analytics cannot be left to statisticians focused on math only

- Skills required of a good data analyst
    - Strategic thinking
    - Knowledge of psychology and people
    - Knowledge of digital technologies
    - Causal mindset - being able to diagnose a business driver
    - Creative problem solving

- Data > Information > Knowledge > Wisdom

Good analytical skills frequently go with good strategic thinking skills, knowledge of psychology and people, good product knowledge, and a causal mindset (or the ability to diagnose a cause that may not be numerical but cultural and/or circumstantial). This is why many top CEOs are frequently known for being very analytical—you need that skill (and some others) to lead a complex business.

A good business/data analyst in the 21st century needs to be effective on the continuum of skills from data collection, translating it to information, supplementing it with business knowledge, and ultimately, the wisdom to know how to apply digital technology to increase profits.

- Good analytical skills are stepping stones to
  - Digital product and service designers
  - Chief Digital Officers
  - CEOs

Good business data analysts are also usually creative problem solvers. The combination of their business knowledge with the knowledge of data and digital technologies makes them good candidates for designers of new digital products and services.

A successful career as a business data analyst is a great stepping stone to the executive suite. A very good business analyst will most likely keep an eye on the corner office, hoping to become a Chief Digital Officer in the future.

Thus, if you are dreaming of an executive suite in a complex, 21st-century business, start now by mastering business data analysis skills. :-)

The value of good data cannot be overestimated. It could mean the difference between life and death, or between bankruptcy and profitable growth.

Analytics - Digital Gold Mine

Jet planes are a perfect example of data's impact on life and death decisions. Pilots fly combat jets by wire—they rely on instruments, or data, to make critical decisions. Wrong or missing data may mean flight termination. Good and early data detection of enemy aircraft may mean survival.

A big bank in Chicago, over 20 years ago, did not know the distribution of its own loan volume by industry and was not aware of the risk exposure when that industry experienced a serious downturn. It happened that a significant part of their lending portfolio was in that sector. This bank is no longer around.

In business, good data may be worth billions. Just ask Google and Facebook.

- Flying by wire
- Bankruptcy by ignorance
- Value of good business data

Analytics, Data Mining, Business Intelligence, Data Visualization, Executive Dashboards

Analytics, Data Mining, Business Intelligence, Data Visualization, Executive Dashboards, Decision Support Systems, and OLAP are all interchangeable marketing terms for using software to analyze data and come up with managerial reports, charts, and alerts. While jockeying for market position, vendors come up with all these new terms, which causes a lot of confusion.

Today, all data analytics vendors provide 99 percent of the same functionalities. The differences between their systems are like the difference between Toyota and Honda. All of them do a decent job analyzing data.

The limit of analytics is not in the different functionality of tools from different vendors. They are all very similar. The limit of data analysis is in data relevance and quality as well as in the analytical skills of users. We will elaborate on this later in this section.

- Managerial
  - Reports
  - Chart
  - Alerts

- Most analytical software has very similar functionality
- The limit is not in analytical software tools
  - Data quality issues
  - Analytical skills

Analytics - Monitoring

These were three extreme examples to make a point. In most businesses, the impact of good, bad, or missing data is generally not that immediate or severe. After all, these businesses have functioned without perfect data so far.

Nevertheless, good granular data allows for the detailed monitoring of processes to increase efficiency and effectiveness. Monitoring is the first basic step. Without good data and analytics, we may have been flying by the seat of our pants, using gut feelings and experience, or just old fashioned guesstimating.

Even just basic monitoring can bring a lot of value. We know who sold what and when to whom for how much and we get daily updates on variance from the budget, so we are not surprised at month-end that we did not meet the target.

In manufacturing, we know what machine produced what product, who worked on what shift, and the actual quantity and cost of inputs. In logistics, we know what was shipped where, how long it took, and where all the trucks are at any given time. For monitoring, we need basic descriptive analytics such as minimum, maximum, mean, median, mode, and variance.

Good quality monitoring is required, but it's not a sufficient basis for the type of process automation that can lead to substantial savings in labor costs, for example.

- Monitoring as a first step
- No surprises
- Basic descriptive analytics
  - Minimum
  - Maximum
  - Mean
  - Median
  - Variance
- Good monitoring can enable automation

Data > Information > Monitoring > Automation > Optimization

After we collected all the data, translated it to information that enabled monitoring, and automated our processes, the next frontier was to optimize it.

Optimization

- How much I did, how much I spent
- Did I do the best job with respect to:
  - Goals
  - Costs
  - Quality
  - Time constraints, etc.
- Soil irrigation

Manufacturing provides a lot of good examples of process optimization. It's one thing to know how much I produced and how much I spent. It's another thing to know whether I did the best job I could. Maybe too much energy was used, maybe a slight increase in the quality of input can greatly improve outcomes, maybe I should be cooling or heating the process sooner or later.

With the collection of relevant and sufficiently detailed data, we can answer these questions. We can not only monitor but also optimize the process. For optimization, basic prescriptive statistics are not enough; we need to use sophisticated algorithms.

A good example of process optimization is soil irrigation. Water management is crucial in many parts of the world and even a 10 percent reduction in unnecessary usage can make a big difference.

Based on real-time data about the type of soil, its moisture and temperature as well as ambient air temperature and humidity, and time of a day, a sprinkler turns itself on and dispenses the right amount of water, then shuts itself down. The algorithm that is used calculates the minimum amount of water for the desired soil moisture, given factors that impact that moisture. In this case, ambient temperature and humidity impact evaporation, which prevents a certain percentage of water from sinking into the ground.

Predictive Analytics

- Credit card fraud detection
- Predicting equipment failure
- Automatic shutdown

There are several sophisticated applications of real-time analytics, especially when applied to voluminous amounts of real-time data. The fancy new term is Predictive Analytics. From an analytical perspective, it's just a lot of real-time analytics based on an algorithm written by someone very familiar with the process.

This includes credit card fraud detection in the financial world or predicting equipment failure in manufacturing.

In the case of credit card fraud detection, historical patterns of charges are compared with real-life charges. If a customer has been charging 99 percent of their transactions over the last two years in stores with zip codes around their home and the highest single transaction never exceeded $2,000, then predictive analytics software will flag an attempt to charge $15,000 in an overseas store 8,000 miles away.

Another good example of predictive analytics is predicting equipment failure. One can do it by measuring an engine's vibration and/or input of energy. From the previous analysis, it's known that a certain ratio or level of vibration to increased energy consumption indicates a mechanical problem with bearings. When this ratio is measured in real-time and exceeds the predefined level, the software sends an alert (text or email) flagging the need for service or replacement of critical equipment. The software can also send a signal to an automatic process controller to shut the whole operation down. This logic is determined by the plant's operational managers.

The Achilles Heel Of Analytics

The Achilles heel of business analytics is neither the amount of data we collect nor the lack of statistical models or predictive algorithms.

Rather, it's related to these three phenomena:

1. Lack of relevant data (not collected at all and/or not granular enough)
2. Poor data integrity
3. Lack of compatibility

If we do not collect weight every day we will never be able to know how many pounds a patient lost or gained last week. This may sound trivial, but collecting more frequent or more granular data costs time and money, and decisions need to be made as to the value of such a discovery. However, it seems to us that the cost of weighing a patient daily is much less than the cost of readmissions that could have been prevented if the data revealed a problem much sooner.

Another example is our current weather prediction systems. We do not collect enough granular data about wind, temps, humidity, precipitation, etc. to be able to predict the weather in the next 24 hours with 99 percent certainty. To be that accurate, we would need to have many more weather stations installed and feed the data in real time, but this is still too expensive. So we live with imperfection, as perfection is too expensive.

The last example is data relevance. If you do not collect the data that drives things that you try to measure, you may never be able to explain what is going on.

Let's discuss a simple scenario. You do not collect data on food or drug allergies (or it is not readily available). You admit a patient and prescribe drugs that a patient is allergic to or serve food he should not consume. A patient experiences unexplained complications and a very long recovery. A year later, an analyst is trying to understand drivers of extended hospital stays. The analyst is faced with an impossible task because the basic data is not available.

- Poor data quality
  - missing
  - incorrect
  - duplicate
  - not timely
- Garbage in - garbage out

Many businesses today struggle with basic data integrity (missing, incorrect, duplicate, or untimely data). This is typical when data is entered manually. For example, customer names may be misspelled or appear multiple times, phone numbers and some diagnosis info is missing, addresses and gender representations are not collected. Therefore, it would be hard to come up with a simple correct analysis of admissions by day, by diagnosis, by gender, by city, and by household, for example.

There is no escape from the old adage— 'garbage in, garbage out'.

In today's global and competitive economy, one needs to be able to analyze data across multiple systems for conclusive profitability analysis, starting from a marketing campaign, through revenues, procedures, treatments, departments, and customer service. The lack of such information will prevent optimal pricing and resource allocation.

However, today, most marketing departments struggle to even understand the first step. Data from web traffic, email campaigns, online advertising, social media, and actual sales is in five separate systems that frequently don't 'talk' to each other. Therefore, we cannot determine which digital marketing channel is most effective and efficient, despite having all the detailed data paid for and stored on our systems.

This is a simple example of when the drivers are known, but the data is not collected. There is yet another problem when the drivers are unknown but we have a hypothesis that needs to be verified. This is where sophisticated statistics would fit in, and this is beyond the scope of our discussion.

> Not everything that can be counted counts,
> and not everything that counts can be
> counted.
>
> *-Unknown*

Measuring business activities is not without cost. Even if data storage cost is negligible, there is the cost of the technical staff's setting up systems to collect, cleanse, and organize the data, and then there is the cost of expensive knowledge workers to perform such analysis.

It is management's responsibility (with the input from data analysts) to decide what data needs to be collected and to determine that it's worth analyzing. As this quote says, not everything that can be counted counts, and not everything that counts can be counted.

We can count the number of grains of sand in a sandbox, but what is the point? And we cannot count friendship or loyalty, which counts a lot.

Summary - Analytics

- A crucial skill for 21st-century executives
- Digitization means measuring more and better
- More measurement > More data collected
- Data is useless unless turned into information

- Information is useless unless it is supported by business knowledge
- Knowledge is useless if it is not wisely applied to make a profit or improve the outcome
- Measurement leads to better monitoring
- Monitoring enables automation
- Automation enables optimization
- Optimization means higher profits

Security And Privacy
Digital Achilles Heel

So far we have painted a very optimistic picture of the digital revolution's having a profound impact on economic growth.

However, in addition to the data integrity issues we discussed earlier, there are two other looming issues of even higher severity and importance. They are data security and privacy.

Security and privacy are completely intertwined; there is no privacy without security. However, privacy can be violated even with the best security when the right privacy policies are not in place.

- Utmost importance
- Security vs. convenience
- People are the biggest vulnerability

- Mitigate risk - risk will always be there
- Continuous problem - cannot just be fixed one time

Security is of the utmost importance. Only with good security solutions will the adoption of all these great digital concepts move forward to benefit our society. Otherwise, business managers will hesitate to take on so much risk.

Security is both a technical and organizational challenge. We need to balance convenience with safety. Too much security will slow down transactions and thus economic development. Too little security will have a similarly chilling effect on the economy as people will not engage as much as they would if they felt safe.

People are the weakest link in security. Disgruntled, careless, or untrained employees account for most security breaches.

Therefore, the risk of security breaches will always be there. It can be managed and mitigated, but it cannot be eliminated. This is a continuous problem—it cannot be fixed at one time.

As long as humans are involved, there will be security challenges. After all, the history of humankind is also a history of inventing the best locks and the corresponding lockpicks.

Privacy - Digital Right To Be Left Alone

Privacy issues will have to be dealt with via legislation. We already have a precedent in the U.S. with respect to the privacy of our medical records. These privacy provisions are captured and enforced by HIPAA regulations (The Health Insurance Portability and Accountability Act of 1996).

We see no technical reason why the same protection cannot be extended to our personal data that we ourselves generate while interacting on the Internet. Every one of us should have a right to opt in or out of our own personal data sharing with various Internet providers and expect that these providers will honor the agreement under the penalty of law.

After all, the content of our regular mail is not available to the U.S. Post Office for sale. By putting our paper letters in a sealed envelope and affixing a postage stamp, we enter into an explicit contract with the Post Office that the privacy of our content is protected and won't be snooped on. If anybody gets caught opening and reading our old-fashioned paper letters, they will end up in a state penitentiary as opposed to enriching themselves selling our private information.

In a May 2014 ruling by the Court of Justice of the European Union, the court decided that users have the right to ask search engines like Google to remove results for queries that include their name. To qualify, the results shown would need to be inadequate, irrelevant, no longer relevant, or excessive. This ruling, however, does not apply to public figures.

We believe that this is a move in the right direction. We should have full rights to opt in and opt out of sharing our personal information, and that right should be strictly enforced.

We have the rights to our private property and we can trade them on the market. There is no reason we cannot do the same with the information we authored ourselves. As HIPAA shows, this is doable.

It may involve some costs, but the social media giants have plenty of cash to pay for such protection. They made this money by selling our personal information to advertisers, so it should be their responsibility to guard it and to be severely punished when they breach that trust. After all, hacking is a crime today.

In another development, The United States House of Representatives is currently working on the

Intimate Privacy Protection Act, a bipartisan bill that would make it illegal to distribute explicit private images without the consent of the people involved. It would stipulate criminal punishment for third parties who profit from the sale of such material. The bill was prompted by Gawker's publishing private erotic videos of Hulk Hogan. This is another step in the right direction. The law is slowly catching up with the digital revolution. **Patient data should belong to and be controlled by the patient and shared with health providers at the patient's discretion.**

- Legislation and enforcement is the only answer
- HIPAA precedence
- Protection for personal data as for medical records
- Right to be removed
- Intimate Privacy Protection Act

- Cloud Computing
- Internet of Things IoT
- RFID
- API
- AR & VR
- Artificial Intelligence
- Machine Learning
- Voice To Text
- Big Data
- Data Warehouse
- Blockchain
- Analytics
- Privacy and Security

11
Call to Action

Just Digitize It

We have demonstrated the Smart Healthcare vision and how to implement it by using unique Patient Experience Quotient (PEQ) methodology. PEQ is also a great communication tool to build consensus and support among C-suites, boards, and foundations as well as regulators.

Nevertheless:

- Vision without action is just a dream.
- Action without vision is just chaos.
- Only the right vision combined with the right actions will make a difference and lead to increased productivity and profitability.

Few people like to change. Change is very hard to accept in the short run. However, not changing will make things even harder in the long run.

The competition is not sleeping. The only way to compete in the 21st century is to do the right things very well and very fast. Effective change always calls for a very detailed mapping of the current and future processes.

In healthcare, there are only three competitive weapons: a) improving outcomes, b) increasing productivity via better processes, and c) maintaining superior patient experience, including timely communication with your customers on their terms. This translates into doing more with less. The only way to accomplish that is to digitize your healthcare business to have real-time insights.

Without such improvements, you may lose your business to those who are willing and able to change and digitize their operations.

Just Digitize It!

Call 904.999.8826 or visit 3clicks.us
or email info@3clicks.us for a
free 1-hour consultation on how to assess your
PEQ.

ABOUT THE AUTHORS

CHARLES BELL

Charles is a seasoned entrepreneur with more than 35 years of healthcare technology experience. He is one of the first pioneers of digitizing the Patient Experience. Charles has founded, cofounded and managed several successful national and international healthcare technology companies including Angelwatch, Dwyer Precision Products, Westside Communications, Wescom (Intego), Bellco Ventures and Linxio Group.

In the early 1980's he saw the need to form Wescom) an international design and manufacturing company focused on using software base technology to automate the process and delivery of patient care needs. **He formed a team and led the development of a patient-centric communications platform that included nurse to patient communication, locating, tracking, EMR integration and analytics. The focus was to** provide a safe and quiet environment, improve care provider efficiency while delivering a better patient outcome.

In 1984 he installed his first Central Command Center (Virtual Care Center) focused on delivering the best Patient Experience. The system allowed to manage all patient related communications (alerts , alarms, and requests from one central point. The virtual command center increased efficiency provided a quieter environment without the need to add staff, increase the number of work hours while also increasing patient satisfaction and providing a better patient outcome.

In 2006, he rebranded Wescom as Intego. Currently more than 200 healthcare facilities worldwide are using the technology. In February of 2012 he negotiated the sale of the assets of Intego to Critical Alert (www.criticalalert.com) and became an equity partner in Critical Alert and was appointed the role as Chief Strategy and Business Development Officer. He held this position from 2012-mid 2013. His customers include among others:

- Lakeland Regional Health
- Boca Raton Regional Hospital
- Baptist Health
- Lakeland Regional Health
- Methodist Le Bonheur Healthcare

- Ascension Health
- Nationwide Children's
- Ohio Health
- UFHealth
- Duke University
- South Georgia Medical Center
- OSF HealthCare
- Corniche Hospital – United Arab Emirates

Charles is currently a principal in several healthcare technology companies that provide cloud-based software solutions and professional services to clients throughout the U.S. Below are several companies where he currently has ownership and/or management responsibility:

- Critical Alert
- Dr. Connection Benefits, LLC
- Legacy Strategy Group, LLC
- Linxio Group, LLC
- Bellco Ventures, LLC

Charles also served as a member of the University of North Florida Brooks College of Health Dean's Council and the Brooks College of Health Advancement Committee for more than ten years.

He is also an inventor with several patents.

- Patent: U.S. Pat. No. 5,426,425

A locating and monitoring system that includes transmitters worn by a person, animal, or equipment to transmit a unique identification code while moving about a facility.

- Patent: U.S. Pat No. 5,957,603

Combination support and eraser for a dry-erase marker.

Connect with Charles on LinkedIn at
https://www.linkedin.com/in/charlesbellsr/

GREG GUTKOWSKI

Digital Strategist & Bestselling Author. Greg has over 20 years of multi-disciplinary global business experience spanning marketing, sales, and IT management, as well as Internet software development, IoT, advanced data analytics, and journalism.

Greg has earned the following advanced degrees: MBA in IT Management, MS in Economics, MS in Journalism.

He currently runs the business education company 3CLICKS.US. Greg teaches business analytics and digital strategies at the University of North Florida Coggin College of Business where he is a member of the Marketing Advisory Board.

Greg has worked over the years with customers from various industries. He has helped with his analytics and marketing expertise, among others:

Allstate, American Express, Aon/Hewitt, AT Kearney, AT&T, Aurora Healthcare, Blue Cross Blue Shield of Illinois, Charmer-Sunbelt, Continental Bank, Dean Foods, Exxon-Mobil, First Bank, John Alden Life, Ralph Polo, United Stationers, and the University of North Florida.

He has also designed analytics systems for several K-12 public and private school districts across the U.S. to assist them in evaluating the effectiveness of various education programs. His analytic software has been implemented by many leading U.S. school districts.

As a young man, Greg moved to the United States as a political refugee from the former communist empire of the Soviet Union. Since his teenage years in his native Poland, he has always been inspired by the uniquely American idea of the pursuit of happiness being a foundation of the U.S. Constitution. Greg believes that such a dream can only be achieved via economic and personal freedoms supported by transparent measurements.

Connect with Greg on LinkedIn at
https://www.linkedin.com/in/greggutkowski

Other books by Greg available on Amazon:

Digital Business – How to Sharpen Your Executive Skills

Digital Tsunami – How to Thrive in the 21st Century

9 Best Kept Secrets of B2B Digital Marketing

The Measurement Revolution – How to Thrive with Digital Analytics

21st Century Marketing - How to Blend Digital and Traditional Methods

21st Century Subcontracting – How to Run Your Whole Construction Business from Your Smartphone